D1544896
Newmill
TRING
TRING PARK
CHILTERN HILL
Hastoe
Wick Wood
High Scrubs
Pavis Wood
North hill Wood
Buckland Wood
St. Leonard's Common
Buckland Common
Cholesbury
CHOLESBURY
Acres
178·142
Stonehill Wood
Terrier's End
West Leith

The Country of Larks

A Chiltern Journey

Gail Simmons

THE COUNTRY OF LARKS

A Chiltern Journey

In the Footsteps of
Robert Louis Stevenson
and the Footprint of HS2

GAIL SIMMONS

Bradt

First published in the UK in April 2019 by Bradt Travel Guides Ltd
IDC House, The Vale, Chalfont St Peter, Bucks SL9 9RZ, England
www.bradtguides.com

Print edition published in the USA by The Globe Pequot Press Inc,
PO Box 480, Guilford, Connecticut 06437-0480

Edited by Tricia Hayne
Proofread by Tom Jordan
Designed by Pepi Bluck, Perfect Picture
Cover linocut illustration by James Green
Illustration of beech tree © grop/Shutterstock.com
Layout and typesetting by Pepi Bluck, Perfect Picture
Route map by David McCutcheon FBCart.S
Endpapers: Ordnance Survey Buckinghamshire XXXIV (includes: Aston Clinton; Buckland; Halton; Wendover) 1883 to 1884, by kind permission of the National Library of Scotland

Production managed by Sue Cooper, Bradt & Jellyfish Print Solutions

ISBN: 978 1 78477 080 8 (print)

British Library Cataloguing in Publication Data
A catalogue record for this book is available from the British Library

Digital conversion by www.dataworks.co.in
Printed in India

About the Author

After a peripatetic army childhood, Gail Simmons settled with her family in a Chiltern village. Like most eighteen year-olds, she couldn't wait to leave home and spread her wings. Decades later – having worked in a Cumbrian castle, listed historic buildings in Warwickshire, led walking groups in Italy and the Middle East, and written for national newspapers – she returned to rediscover the landscape of her youth. Now that the Chilterns are threatened by HS2, she realises how important these modest hills are to her. Gail holds an MA in medieval history and a PhD in creative writing, and teaches travel writing at Bath Spa and Cambridge universities. This is her first book (www.travelscribe.uk).

Acknowledgements

During the writing of this book I have had the great fortune to encounter several people whose passion for the Chiltern landscape has been inspirational. Without them, and their invaluable contributions, this book would not have been possible. They are, in order of appearance, Keith Hoffmeister (Chiltern Society), Alison Doggett (Chiltern historian), Robert Brown (Chiltern farmer), Matthew Jackson (head of conservation, BBOWT) and John Elvin (Chiltern Line Association).

Other kind people have checked facts, read the text or otherwise made helpful suggestions. Among these are Claudia Shaffer (friend and unofficial agent), Stephen Moss (naturalist and author), Clare Best (poet and Chiltern devotee), Laura Littlejohn (transcriber and campaigner), Anita Roy (freelance editor and writer), Christopher North (poet and botanist), Richard Bailey (husband and proofreader), Jill Simmons (mother and proofreader), Neil Jackson (conservation and landscape officer, Chilterns AONB), and Robert Wolton (Hedgelink). I'd also like to thank the RSPB (rspb.org.uk) and Historic England (historicengland.org.uk) for allowing me to quote from their excellent websites.

The definition of place names is not an exact science, and the place names defined in this book are a composite of those found in a variety of sources. These include the *Anglo-Saxon Chronicle*, *Domesday Book* (1086), *A Topographical Dictionary of England* (Samuel Lewis, S Lewis & Co, 1831), *The Concise Oxford Dictionary of English Place-names* (Eilert Ekwall, Clarendon Press, 1960) and *A Dictionary of British Place Names* (A D Mills, Oxford University Press, 1991).

For my parents –

not from the Chilterns, though of the Chilterns

CONTENTS

Overhead there was a wonderful carolling of larks which seemed to follow me as I went. Indeed, during all the time I was in that country the larks did not desert me. The air was alive with them from High Wycombe to Tring; and as, day after day, their 'shrill delight' fell upon me out of the vacant sky, they began to take such a prominence over other conditions, and form so integral a part of my conception of the country, that I could have baptized it 'The Country of Larks'.

R L Stevenson, 'In the Beechwoods', 1875

For my part, I travel not to go anywhere, but to go. I travel for travel's sake. The great affair is to move; to feel the needs and hitches of our life more clearly; to come down off this feather-bed of civilization, and find the globe granite underfoot and strewn with cutting flints.

R L Stevenson, *Travels with a Donkey in the Cévennes*, 1879

HS2 is a high-speed railway under construction in the United Kingdom which, when completed, will connect London, Birmingham, Leeds and Manchester. It will be the second high-speed rail line in Britain, the first being High Speed 1 (HS1), which connects London to the Channel Tunnel.

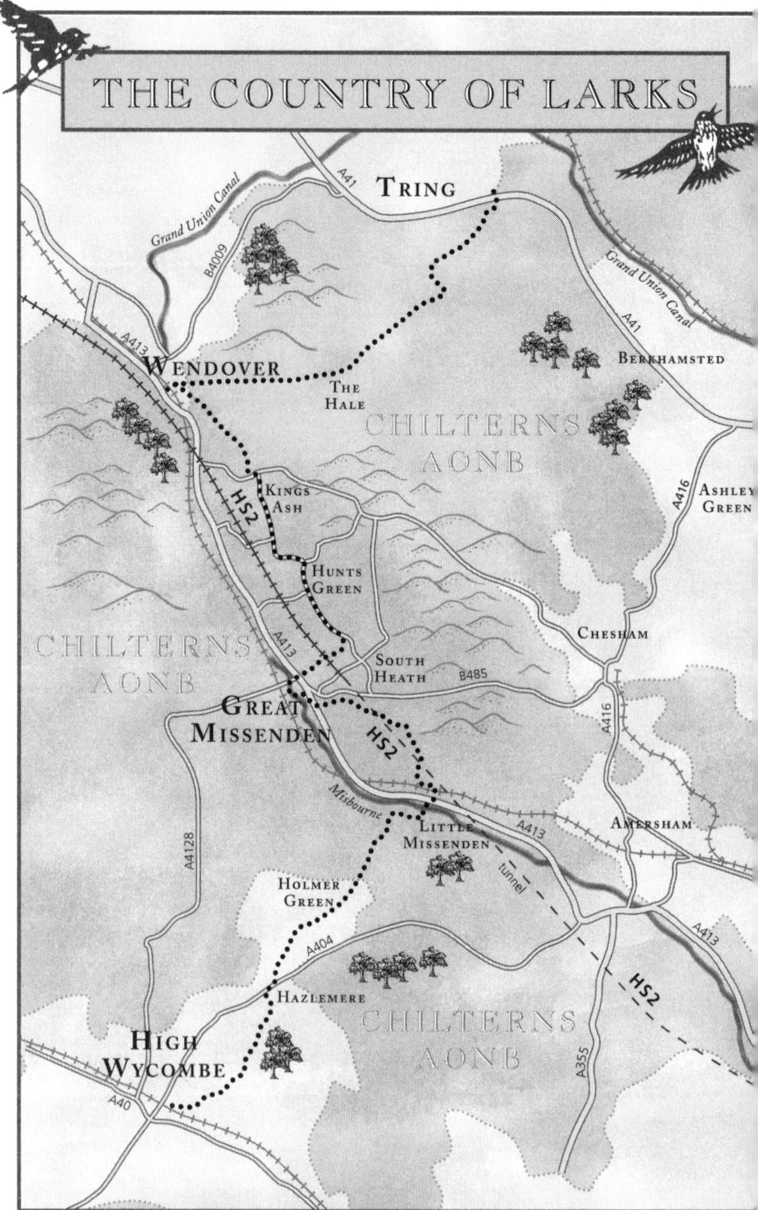
THE COUNTRY OF LARKS
Tring
Grand Union Canal
A41
B4009
Grand Union Canal
A41
A413
Wendover
The Hale
Berkhamsted
Chilterns AONB
Kings Ash
HS2
Hunts Green
A416
Ashley Green
Chesham
Chilterns AONB
A413
South Heath
B485
Great Missenden
HS2
A416
Misbourne
Little Missenden
A413
Amersham
A4128
tunnel
Holmer Green
A404
A413
Hazlemere
HS2
Chilterns AONB
High Wycombe
A355
A40

PROLOGUE

Chiltern: 'hill-slope'; possibly of Brittonic origin, *celto-erno*, Ciltern (1009)

One bright morning in early autumn I set out to walk across the Chiltern Hills, following in the footsteps of the author Robert Louis Stevenson. It was almost 150 years since he had crossed these same hills, arriving in High Wycombe by train and stopping overnight at Great Missenden and Wendover before reaching Tring three days later. In choosing this route he took a shortcut across the chalk escarpment, walking from south to north – a journey of some twenty miles.

Like Stevenson, I arrived in High Wycombe by train. My passage was courtesy of Chiltern Railways, which runs from London Marylebone to the Midlands, passing through the hills after which the line is named. Unlike Stevenson, I knew the landscape of my childhood by heart. Placid hills crowned with woods of beech, ash and oak – well-bred cousins to the thorny uplands and sullen moors of my current Yorkshire habitat. Intimate valleys scooped out by glaciers where clear chalk streams now glide. Narrow lanes and deep holloways, secretive and tunnel-like under canopies of foliage. Flint churches glinting in autumn sunshine, harbouring time-weathered wall paintings within.

Hamlets huddled in secluded dells, or perched high on chalky hills. Villages of russet-roofed cottages clustering around ancient ponds where livestock once drank and ducks now float, serenely. So fixed in my mind's eye is this muted and melodious landscape that I did not need to gaze through the train window as it slipped by. But gaze I did – for the Chilterns was once my home, and this was my homecoming.

When Stevenson arrived at High Wycombe to walk across the Chilterns he was twenty-four. He had yet to find fame with *Treasure Island*, *Kidnapped* and *The Strange Case of Dr Jekyll and Mr Hyde*, all written a decade later. He had not yet even penned his best-known travelogue, *Travels with a Donkey in the Cévennes* (1879). By the time *Essays of Travel*, the book that included an account of his Chiltern walk, was published in 1905[1] he had been dead nearly ten years. At the age of forty-four he is thought to have suffered a cerebral haemorrhage in his home in Samoa in the South Pacific, a world away from the benevolent Chiltern countryside of his youthful wanderings.

My own Chiltern story began in 1969, almost a century after Stevenson's. My father, having retired early from the British Army, chose to install our itinerant family in the Buckinghamshire village of Ashley Green. One of the village's prime attractions was its proximity to Berkhamsted, from where he could commute to London Euston and his new job in the City. But just a few generations back – certainly at the time Robert Louis Stevenson lived – my father, like most of the male population, would have been a farmer. He would have belonged to the land, worked its

1 The essay was originally entitled 'In the Beechwoods' but at the time of its first publication in *Portfolio* magazine in 1875, it was renamed 'An Autumn Effect'.

soil with his hands, wiped the sweat from his brow and scraped the dirt from his fingernails. Finely in tune with the elements and with each incremental change of season, his whole life, and that of his family, would have depended on a small patch of English ground. Just as we depended now on him – a twentieth-century breadwinner, dutifully commuting to London for twenty years.

But we cannot so easily shake off this deep bond with the earth, and with our own piece of landscape, despite the camouflage of pressed suits and the smokescreen of commuter trains. On summer weekday evenings my father would put down his briefcase and, still in his business suit, head straight out to the garden to look over the borders he'd worked on during the weekends. My memory is of him walking alongside the flowerbeds, his hands clasped behind his back as if inspecting the troops. As our mother put the finishing touches to supper, he would head back outside armed with a watering can. Sometimes I followed him into the stifling greenhouse to inhale the peppery scent of tomatoes. My father seemed to loosen and unravel as he tended the plants, just as the parched leaves did as he sprinkled cool water over them.

For my father, whether he recognised it as such, watering his tomatoes for a few minutes each evening was his way of renewing his bond with the soil, taming his small patch of landscape, reconnecting with the past. He might have spent his own life encased in school uniform, army regimentals and business suits, but once the wrappings of modern life were peeled back he was a countryman to the core. Even now, a quarter of a century into his retirement, my father still seems happiest outside, cultivating the roses in his Chiltern garden.

In the early autumn of 2017, when I decided to follow in Stevenson's footsteps, a new railway line was planned, threatening to consume everything in its path – including the comfortable lives of Chiltern commuters, and of retirees such as my father. HS2 (or High Speed 2 as it's properly known) will run from London Euston to the Midlands, and then on to northern England. It will cut through the Chiltern Hills, above and below ground, bisecting the route taken by Stevenson in 1874. It will not run through my parents' village of Ashley Green, but it will cross the nearby parishes of Wendover, the Chalfonts and the Missendens just a few miles away. Like a Roman road, it will march almost arrow-straight through the heart of the Chilterns Area of Outstanding Natural Beauty (AONB), mowing through the landscape.

Covering 324 square miles and stretching across swathes of Buckinghamshire and Bedfordshire, Hertfordshire and Oxfordshire, the Chilterns AONB is recognised as a landscape of national importance. Yet with HS2, ancient woodlands, historic buildings, centuries-old field systems and long-standing boundaries will be sacrificed. Grim's Ditch, a Bronze and Iron Age earthwork named after a Norse war god, will be severed. Despite its status as a scheduled monument, a 150-metre stretch will be destroyed. My mother, not normally very political, is rather upset about it. I'm upset about it too, even though I left the Chilterns long ago.

And it's not only this new railway line that endangers the natural and built heritage of the Chilterns. Creeping urbanisation, intensive farming and population pressures are transforming the landscape at a startling rate. For Robert Louis Stevenson, despite the recent industrial revolution and the Enclosure Acts, the country he passed through had changed little for centuries. Reading 'In the Beechwoods', his essay about his Chiltern walk, instils a sense of timelessness of countryside and of culture. For me, writing a century and a half later, the impression of a fast-disappearing landscape is overwhelming. The idyllic panorama glimpsed from my train window exists chiefly in my mind's eye, living on in memory only.

Even in the few decades since I lived in Ashley Green, just a few miles from Tring where Stevenson ended his journey, the change has been palpable. Since I grew up here in the 1970s, farmland birds have declined in number by half, reflecting a trend in wildlife worldwide, as highlighted in a recent report by the WWF. The magnificent elm, beloved of poets from John Clare to John Betjeman, has virtually disappeared from our islands, and the ash – like the beech so characteristic of the Chiltern landscape – threatens to follow. Until recently I wouldn't have been able to describe an ash tree. Now I see them everywhere. In my home of Ashley Green they were once so numerous the village was named after a clearing in their midst:

Ashley: 'ash wood or clearing in an ash wood';
from Old English *æsc* + *leah*

In undertaking this walk I hoped to trace not only the changes this small sliver of England has seen since Stevenson's time, but also how it has changed since I lived here forty years ago. Moreover, I wanted to record what will – if progress has its way – be further lost to us with HS2. As I write, the 'enabling works' have begun (although the discovery of prehistoric artefacts near

Great Missenden has delayed activity there) and the mild hills and dells of my Chiltern childhood will be altered irrevocably. So this is a pilgrimage in honour of Robert Louis Stevenson the travel writer, but also in honour of a land – my land – that was once so rich and diverse, so bursting with birdsong, that Stevenson named it 'The Country of Larks'.

The Campaigner

It was a few days before my walk when Keith Hoffmeister opened the front door of his bungalow in Little Chalfont, a prosperous commuter village in the heart of the Buckinghamshire Chilterns. He led me into a sunlit sitting room where patio doors opened out onto a garden glowing with late summer colour. It was his wife, Keith told me, who was responsible for the garden's charm. Keith himself was too busy with his own projects, as an active member of the Chiltern Society and of the pressure group Stop HS2.

Before he retired Keith Hoffmeister was in insurance. These days his main hobby is photography. 'That's how you get involved in things,' he told me. 'People ask me, can you take pictures of this, can you take pictures of that?' In 2016 Keith spent three days in a small plane, taking aerial photographs of the HS2 route from London to Birmingham. 'I think I know the route better than anybody else,' he said. I told him I'd only ever seen it indicated on maps, where it's hard to visualise. But seeing it marked on these photographs, crossing real fields and through real villages, brought it starkly to life.

We sat down at a table overlooking the garden where Keith had spread out maps, photographs and sheaves of documents. I showed him my own map marked with the route of my walk, and Keith studied it closely.

'It's going to be tunnelled from the M25 at Denham all the way to here, just beyond South Heath.' He placed his finger to where the words Moat and Enclosure are shown in Gothic script, this being the Ordnance Survey convention for an antique site. South Heath is a village I'd be passing through on foot in a few days' time. He traced a line right across my map with his finger, showing the planned route of the train. My walk was neatly bisected by HS2.

'Many people have already moved away from South Heath,' Keith told me. 'A lot of the properties have been bought by HS2 and are let out, but the village will never be the same. The community has been split apart.' He then pointed to a footpath that leads up from Great Missenden in the valley to South Heath on the hill. 'This will be a temporary haul road, and one of the first things that will be built in this area. That will give access from the tunnel portal, so all the construction traffic will come along the A413 then up that footpath.' It was exactly the route I was planning to take out of Great Missenden, on day two of my walk.

When it emerges from the tunnel, HS2 will continue along a deep cutting through the Misbourne Valley, then travel over a short section of viaduct, passing Wendover. It will leave the Chilterns AONB just northwest of the town.

The Misbourne ('bourne' derives from the Old English, *burna*, meaning 'spring') is a shallow chalk stream, characteristic of the Chilterns, which rises just above Great Missenden and flows through Little Missenden,

Old Amersham and the Chalfonts, joining the River Colne near Denham. It follows, almost exactly, the route of HS2. Bled almost dry from its aquifers by water companies, by the 1980s the Misbourne was listed amongst the top British rivers most affected by abstraction. It was rescued in recent years by campaigners, who persuaded the water companies to find more sustainable sources. The river is still vulnerable in times of drought, or from disturbances to the impermeable layer under the porous chalk-stream bed from infrastructure projects such as HS2.

'Why can't they just tunnel under the whole of the AONB?' I asked Keith. 'Too expensive?'

'Some of the groups that have done an enormous amount of work on this reckon it won't cost much more, if anything,' replied Keith. 'We had a lovely morning with the House of Commons Select Committee, and did a walk with them all round this part of the valley. I was very impressed with the MPs, marching in their suits through this historic woodland. But why they decided to stop the tunnel at South Heath, and not go all the way under the AONB, I have no idea.'

'So do you feel that all your lobbying and campaigning has made any difference at all?'

'Definitely, though it hasn't stopped HS2 happening, and it hasn't significantly changed the route, which was a desktop exercise. Basically, they drew a straight line between London and Birmingham because they want this train to go at 250 miles per hour. And a straight line from London to Birmingham goes through the middle of an AONB.'

'Or under it,' I countered.

'Or under it. But there are other routes which would have been much better altogether, like alongside the M1. One of the reasons the route goes this way was that it was supposed to connect with Heathrow. That's not going to happen now. It was also going to link to HS1, the high-speed train from St Pancras to the Channel Tunnel, so you could get on in Manchester and get off in Paris. That's not going to happen either.'

'And it's not even going into Birmingham New Street Station, I understand.'

'No, it will drop people off at Moor Street. So the half-hour you've saved on the journey you're going to waste getting into the middle of Birmingham. But this precious half-hour they touted: it's been dropped now because they realise that business people – and this is who we're talking about – are not particularly bothered about saving a bit of time. They want a regular, reliable service that allows them to work on the train, because that's factored into their working day. They know they've got an hour or whatever to sit on the train, and not be disturbed.'

'A kind of high-speed office?'

'Very much so. HS2's business case was that time on a train is time wasted. But it's an absolute fallacy. The time supposedly saved gave what they call a benefit-cost ratio of about two. That was pie in the sky, and that business case came down and down. Once it comes down to nearly level, one-to-one, then red lights go on. Is this going to provide value for money? Well, those red lights have been flashing for a long time. But no-one listens, because they've got this fixation, and no-one wants to lose face.'

'So is there anyone around here who does think HS2 is a good idea?' If there was a counter view, I wanted to know about it.

'No-one in the Chilterns is going to benefit, because there aren't going to be any stations here. Nobody here can use it without going into London first. And if they're going to Birmingham they're going to travel by car, which defeats the whole object of this super-duper high-speed train.'

If all goes to plan, Keith told me, construction would be due to start in early 2019. I recalled the protests in the mid-1990s, when thousands of people demonstrated against the Newbury bypass, with hundreds arrested. 'Do you think people will actually protest?' I asked him.

'I don't think so. In the early days a lot of people said, "I'll chain myself to a tree." But I don't think that the people in this area would do that sort of thing. And it's a bit pointless anyway, as by the time you've got that far it's going to happen. So you may get yourself arrested and on TV, but unfortunately it's not going to stop it.'

We talked a little about the ancient roads, tracks and boundaries, such as Grim's Ditch near South Heath (another site that earns the Ordnance Survey Gothic treatment), which will be damaged by HS2. There are so many old routes crossing this small area of the Chilterns: the Ridgeway, the Icknield Way, Akeman Street.

'I grew up around here, and I couldn't wait to escape boring old Ashley Green,' I told Keith as I got up to leave.

'As a teenager you don't realise what you have on your doorstep. You just don't appreciate it. But when you hear about this sort of thing it makes you re-evaluate what you had, and everything you are about to lose.'

On my way out I stopped to admire Mrs Hoffmeister's sun-drenched garden again, wondering if Mr Hoffmeister found any time between his campaigning and photography to spend in it.

'It must be very hard not to get obsessed by this HS2 thing,' I remarked as he showed me to the door.

'True, it can take over your life,' he agreed. 'But on the other hand I've met people I never would have otherwise. This campaign has created an amazing sense of community all along the route.'

DAY ONE

High Wycombe
to
Great Missenden

> I begin my little pilgrimage in the most enviable of all humours: that in which a person, with a sufficiency of money and a knapsack, turns his back on a town and walks forward into a country of which he knows only by the vague report of others.

Wycombe: 'settlement, village, dwelling';
from Old English wicum, *Wicumbe* (1086)

In October 1874, a slender young Scotsman carrying a rucksack stepped off the London train onto the platform at High Wycombe station. He was twenty-four, suffering from poor health and in the throes of an unhappy love affair with an older, married woman. Having based himself in London over the summer to be near the object of his affections, and to immerse himself in literary life, Robert Louis Stevenson was now procrastinating over returning to Edinburgh to resume his university studies.

Wearing his favourite velvet jacket, and with his wispy moustache and unkempt hair, the aspiring author must have cut a strikingly bohemian figure in High Wycombe. This was, after all, a respectable working town famed chiefly for the chair-making industry that flourished thanks to the beech woodland covering its nearby hills. The daintier crafts of lace-making and straw-plaiting also thrived here, but from the late eighteenth century it was chairs – particularly good, solid Windsor chairs – that concerned the town's inhabitants. Passing through in 1822, William Cobbett described Georgian High Wycombe as 'a very fine and very clean market town'. By the time that Stevenson alighted here some fifty years later, the rows of terraced workers' cottages had already begun crawling up the steep slopes of the Wye Valley.

Now, almost 150 years on from Stevenson's arrival, I too alighted the train at High Wycombe station. Built in the Chiltern vernacular style of knapped flint with brick dressings, the station had opened just twenty years before Stevenson turned up. This was the heyday of Victorian engineering, a time dominated by names such as Isambard Kingdom Brunel and Robert Louis' own grandfather, the Scottish civil engineer Robert Stevenson. Stevenson the younger, under pressure to follow in his grandfather's and father's footsteps, studied engineering at Edinburgh University with a view to joining the family business. Not showing much promise as an engineer, he then turned to law before abandoning both professions for more artistic pursuits.

Like Stevenson, I too had a rucksack on my back that day. In it I was carrying a pair of 1:25,000 Ordnance Survey maps of the Chilterns, plus – courtesy of the National Library of Scotland

– photocopies of OS maps of the area drawn in the 1880s. The workmanship on these six-inch maps is astounding, with every field, every farm, almost every tree depicted with great care – even love. Surveyed between 1874 and 1877, the maps show the countryside exactly as it must have appeared when Stevenson walked here. But they were not much use to me as I exited the station and looked around. I wasn't even sure which way was north and, embarrassingly for this modest expedition, had to refer to the compass on my smartphone to get my bearings. How on earth could I be lost in the twenty-first century in the centre of a middle-sized town in Middle England?

Stevenson may have had a compass too, though all he needed to do was look up to see his way ahead. After all, he was travelling before the sprawling ribbon development of the 1930s replaced the dilapidated Victorian terraces, enveloping the surrounding hills in housing estates. Or perhaps, like me, he stopped a passer-by to ask for directions to King's Wood – a tract of forest on the high ground to the north of the town. The first person I asked shrugged: he didn't live here. The second, a young man, unplugged himself from his earphones and pointed vaguely up the hillside. The hill turned out to be a web of housing, but the road still winding its intuitive way through forgotten fields and along forsaken boundaries corresponded to the one indicated on my 1880s map, so on I plodded.

An elderly lady in a raincoat was waiting at a bus stop.

'Excuse me, do you live here?' I found myself asking for the third time that morning. A flash of suspicion in her eyes, a moment to sum up whether this stranger in mud-caked walking boots and shabby rucksack posed a threat. But she did live here, and yes, she thought I was walking in the right direction for King's Wood so I climbed on, more confidently now. When Stevenson passed through High Wycombe almost everyone he saw would have lived in the town, and would have known King's Wood. A century on and we are so disconnected from our natural surroundings that most of us would be hard-pushed to name the natural features – the woods, hills and streams – that were as familiar to our forebears as their own neighbours.

> It was well, perhaps, that I had this first enthusiasm to encourage me up the long hill above High Wycombe; for the day was a bad day for walking at best, and now began to draw towards afternoon, dull, heavy, and lifeless.

Stevenson's frame of mind might have coloured his view of the countryside when he passed this way in 1874, his words perhaps describing his own melancholy mood as much as the weather. But I shared his 'first enthusiasm', and it was with an assured stride that I climbed further up the hill leaving the town below, its once organic market-town layout now obliterated by modern roads.

In 1937, High Wycombe was described in Clough Williams-Ellis' classic polemic against urban expansion, *Britain and the Beast*, as 'honestly, if tawdrily, industrial'. Development in the 1960s expanded the town further. This fragmented straggle is how I remember High Wycombe when, in the 1970s, I lived within twelve miles of the town. I never much bothered coming here. Now, High Wycombe could be Damascus for how well I knew my way around it. Indeed, I know my way around Damascus rather better.

Past Bowerdean Road – its name the only remnant of a farm that once sat alone on this chalk-flint hillside, demolished to make way for housing in the 1930s – and along Totteridge Road, which once led to Totteridge Farm. Both settlements, according to my 1880s map, were well out of town. But like Bowerdean Farm, Totteridge Farm today exists in name only, the road leading now to Totteridge Common. Scattered alongside the common, amongst the 1960s suburbs, are survivals from when Totteridge was a village in its own right. The same Chiltern vernacular of knapped-flint cottages under red-tiled roofs as my own village, Ashley Green. High Wycombe, although a stranger to me, was conjoined with my past through its landscape and buildings.

> A pall of grey cloud covered the sky, and its colour reacted on the colour of the landscape. Near at hand, indeed, the hedgerow trees were still fairly green, shot through with bright autumnal yellows, bright as sunshine. But a little way off, the solid bricks of woodland that lay squarely on slope and hill-top were not green, but russet and grey, and ever less russet and more grey as they drew off into the distance.

This day, too, was overcast and steel-grey. I didn't know for sure that this was the way that Stevenson took, but he was certainly headed in the same direction, towards Great Missenden. Painfully thin and plagued throughout his life by ill-health, he nevertheless possessed an adventurous spirit – one that was eventually to take him beyond the docile hills of southern England to the Continent, America and the South Pacific. He perhaps chose a lower, less challenging route across the Chilterns, but I was taking the high road. The hill was steep and, as the town's edges frayed, the ache in my calves told me I was about to traverse the escarpment. Unlike the cars that glided effortlessly by I felt the gradient with every step, and even on this quiet Sunday morning diesel discharge clasped the back of my throat.

Nearing the top, as the gradient flattened, the houses seemed to spread themselves out a little more widely and the trees and hedgerows, ruddy with autumnal berries, seemed to breathe a little more easily. I was in High Wycombe still, but walking across the threshold between the urban and the natural world, and my pace quickened. Now I was leaving town there was no need to ask for directions. The landscape was showing me the way. My internal compass, knocked out of whack by the car-centric townscape below, pulled me in the right direction.

Uplifting as it felt to be leaving the town, this semi-urban, semi-rural world was disquieting, bringing with it that familiar twinge of Sunday suffocation that I felt as a teenager growing up in the Home Counties. Our Sundays in Ashley Green were marked by ritual. As the day drew to a close my father would press his business suit ready for his weekly commute into London. My mother, a traditional housewife, did most of the ironing. But my father – perhaps in homage to his army days when he looked after his uniform – always preferred to iron his own suit. With military precision he would lay out the dark, IBM-regulation outfit on the ironing board, covering the area to be pressed with a damp tea towel. Then, iron in hand, he would flatten the cloth into neat, ram-rod creases. He never confided to us how he felt about his life in Civvy Street, but from his often sombre moods I guessed he was not entirely comfortable being an executive in a suit. Perhaps the Sunday ironing rite was, for him, a means of ensuring his new uniform was up to the job, a carapace against sharp-elbowed commuters on the Northern Line.

Catching up with homework in my bedroom upstairs, the hiss of the steam and the rhythmical creak of the ironing board marked the end of the weekend, sounds that accompanied a sinking sensation in the pit of my stomach as school loomed, inescapably.

In Totteridge Conservation Area, where I now found myself, nature is fenced off, labelled, packaged for human consumption. It was here that I encountered another emblem woven through the fabric of my Chiltern upbringing: an egg-yolk yellow sign marked Buckinghamshire County Council Public Footpath.

This one pointed into King's Wood. Although it had been only half an hour since I'd arrived at High Wycombe, the giddying sense of being lost in apparently familiar surroundings lifted as I entered this beech woodland. Woods like this formed the backdrop to my childhood – all those years spent walking the interlacing footpaths of Ashley Green. But although John Betjeman celebrated these characteristic Chiltern woodlands in his 1960 poem 'Summoned by Bells' – 'Metroland beckoned us out to lanes in beechy Bucks' – beech only became the predominant tree here with the rise of the furniture-making industry in High Wycombe in the 1700s. Before this, beech trees were outnumbered by other broad-leaved species such as oak, ash and elm. By the time Stevenson walked here beech was so pervasive that, according to the author and publisher Charles Knight in his 1864–65 autobiography *Passages of a Working Life During Half a Century*, it was referred to as the 'Buckinghamshire weed'. This beechy landscape, so enduring to my childhood eyes, is in reality as mutable as the seas.

The modern road swings away from the woodland but the old route plunges into King's Wood, named they say after Henry III who granted it to the Knights Templar. The footpath which Stevenson perhaps strode along bisected four-thousand acres of woodland. The left-hand side – named St John's Wood on my 1880s map – has now disappeared under housing, and the once separate village of Hazlemere is today engulfed by High Wycombe.

Beech woods are exquisite at any time of year. The bare scaffold of winter, the dazzling iridescence of spring, the dark canopy of summer. And now, at the cusp of the seasons, emerald shimmering into gold. Summer clinging on, but autumn fastening its grip. My boots ground beechmast and acorns – for centuries fodder for family pigs fattened for slaughter, now rotting uneaten in the mud. This wood, today so Sunday-morning quiet, would once have rung with the noise of the itinerant, highly-skilled artisans who set up camp in these woodlands when the Chilterns was still a working landscape. These were the turners, or 'bodgers' who, using a pole-lathe powered by a foot treadle, worked the beech into chair legs for High Wycombe's furniture factories.

Bodger: from Middle English *bocchen,* 'to patch up, mend'

Daniel Defoe, passing through the county on his *Tour Through the Whole Island of Great Britain* in 1725, noted 'a vast quantity of beech wood which grows in the woods of Buckinghamshire more plentiful than in any other part of England for divers uses, particularly chair-makers, and turnery wares'. Bodgers, who have rather undeservedly bequeathed the English language a verb meaning to 'make or repair (something) badly or clumsily', were still a common sight in the late nineteenth century when Stevenson passed this way. By the 1920s, High Wycombe had diversified into making other furniture besides chairs, becoming the second-largest furniture-making town in the country by the mid-twentieth century, and the bodgers had gone. Echoes of the industry's homespun roots still exist in the local football team, Wycombe Wanderers, who are affectionately known as the Chairboys.

The road noise had faded now, and from beyond the trees echoed only the far-off shouts from a Sunday morning football match. Overhead, jets whined as they dipped towards Heathrow, drowning out the birdsong. Another yolk-yellow sign reassured me that I was indeed on a public footpath, safe and sound in beechy Bucks.

Public footpaths such as the one I was treading that morning, along with bridleways and byways, form around 150,000 miles of rights of way in Britain. They were created over centuries, most having developed as links – both between villages and within them – connecting fields, hamlets and farms. With the enclosure of common land from the seventeenth century onwards began the process of legal protection of these established routes, a protection that continues today with county councils technically responsible for their upkeep. Not as the thoroughfares of centuries past, but as 'amenities' for leisure walkers such as myself, these branded with Buckinghamshire County Council signage.

My path ended abruptly at the edge of a smart housing estate but the ancient right of way, inalienable still, continued unswervingly between walls of panel fencing that screened off landscaped gardens against the prying eyes of walkers. Mature trees closed thickly over my head, and I aimed for the splash of daylight at the end of the tunnel. Wildlife, ever resourceful, is not so easily trammelled and some small creature had burrowed under the fencing, following its own immutable right of way despite suburban man's best efforts to keep it out.

Another private road of hedged-off houses, inhabited by entirely new species of animal: hulking Lexus, Mercedes and Range Rovers crouching in their driveways like twenty-first-century dinosaurs. The dream of Betjeman's Metroland abides, and London commuters still seek a fragment of semi-rural England to call their own in the carved-up Buckinghamshire countryside.

But Hazlemere, where I now stood, was once a hamlet of farms and scattered woodland lying two-and-a-half miles northeast of High Wycombe.

On my 1880s map the hamlet is surrounded by cherry orchards, though cherry orchards grow no longer in Hazlemere's fields. Further back still, it was the hazel that gave it importance.

Hazlemere: 'lake or pond where hazels grow';
from Old English *hæsel + mere*

Hazel was revered in Celtic times as the tree of knowledge, and endowed with magical properties. Cutting one down was punishable by death. In the past it was used for making fences and hurdles, and is still used today in water divining.

I passed Old Post Office Cottage, now a private home. We had a post office too, when I was growing up in Ashley Green. The post office was also the village shop where we'd stop on our way home from school to fill paper bags with psychedelic Seventies sweets: sherbet dips with tough, chewy liquorice, marshmallowy Wagon Wheels, rubbery Wine Gums, stretchy Curly Wurlies that tugged at your teeth. Our mother would walk to the 'corner shop', to buy basic groceries and stamps, and to post her letters. That village shop is long gone, converted many years ago into a residential property, its original door bricked up and camouflaged by a dense growth of ivy obliterating all traces of its lowly commercial past.

And it's not only the shop that has disappeared. Once, when cattle still grazed in Ashley Green's meadows and bicycles wobbled down its lanes, the corner shop adjoined a bakehouse, providing bread for the villagers. Bread was one of the few foods not rationed during World War II (this was introduced only in July 1946 and enforced for two years), the villagers supplementing their otherwise meagre wartime diet with home-grown fruit and vegetables and by keeping a few chickens.

> The sun came out before I had been long on my way; and as I had got by that time to the top of the ascent, and was now treading a labyrinth of confined by-roads, my whole view brightened considerably in colour, for it was the distance only that was grey and cold, and the distance I could see no longer.

Unlike Stevenson, I wasn't treading 'by-roads' but the pavement of the A404 from London to Maidenhead. Empty cans of Red Bull, polystyrene KFC cartons and McDonald's burger boxes ('I'm Lovin' It') littered the verge. Even the trees were snagged with ribbons of plastic, like soldiers limping home from the Front, bandages flapping.

For the littering drivers passing through, who rarely step from their cars, Hazlemere must seem a foreign country. Yet when Stevenson walked here, people would have known every inch of land in their parish. They would have ploughed each furrow themselves, laid every hedgerow, built every wall, all by hand. Everything would have been nurtured, cherished. Each field had a name, as did each wood, copse and stream. People would have spent their whole lives within just a few square miles, and would have had an absolute, symbiotic relationship with their landscape, and with one another. They would have known also their surrounding parishes, and the boundaries that lay between them. And every year on Rogation Sunday the community would have come together to 'beat the bounds', walking the parish boundaries to reinforce their bond with the land in a world without maps. Our communities were once deeply connected – not just within themselves but between each other.

Rogation Sunday was as much a part of the religious rural calendar as Advent, which commences each year on the fourth Sunday before Christmas. But whereas children still look forward to the annual Advent calendar, how many people today have even heard of Rogation Sunday? We have forgotten too, it seems, the rhythm of the entwined religious and agricultural year when the community would come together to share the burden of tasks, such as gleaning:

Glean: 'gather leftover grain etc after a harvest';
from Anglo-Norman *glener*

Yet every month my parents walk down their lane in Ashley Green with a large plastic bag, which they fill with the litter thrown from passing traffic. The modern incarnation of gleaning. Civic responsibility – that virtue of the godless age – has replaced those old religious rituals.

A knapped-flint inn ('Pub & Flame Grill') across the road, still hung with baskets of summer begonias, here revealed a rare trace of old village England. Stevenson would have been passing through on open fields by now, but I was following signs along the busy main road to Holmer Green.

Holmer: 'lake or pond in a hollow';
from Old English *hol + mere*, *Holeme* (1208)

Holmer Green. Such a pleasant, English-villagey name. Like my own village of Ashley Green it is redolent of an Anglo-Saxon gathering of houses around a clearing, smoke curling from thatched roofs, evoking a time when dense woodland sheathed the Chiltern Hills. A site was chosen near a source of water, and cleared of trees. Around this clearing the villagers built a scattering of wooden huts housing both animals and people, from which resonated sounds we would barely recognise today: the scrape of flint against bone as skins were cleaned, and the rhythmic grate of quernstones as cereals were ground into flour to make rudimentary bread. Wheat and rye, oats and barley, beans and turnips, leeks and onions were cultivated in the open fields. Several hundred strips of perhaps half an acre each surrounded the villages of *holmere* and *æscleah* one thousand years ago.

The Domesday Book of 1086 refers to Holmer Green as *Holemere*, but of my village of Ashley Green, then a satellite hamlet of the Buckinghamshire parish of Chesham, there is no mention. *Cestreham*, as it was then, belonged to one Brictric of Waddesdon, passing after the Norman Conquest into the hands of Hugh of Bolbec. The assizes of 1227 comment that trees were to be felled at *Esseleie*, possibly for the Sixth Crusade. By 1468 the village was known, as it is today, as *Assheley Grene*. In both *Holemere* and *Esseleie* the moniker 'Green' is a medieval appendage, added when the common land at the centre of the villages was adopted for grazing. Both greens also have ponds, where villagers once watered their animals. Ashley Green's is now much diminished, but Holmer's green and pond were once part of Wycombe Heath, a four-thousand-acre area of common land where 'commoners' enjoyed rights of pasture for their livestock.

Much of the country's common land was lost after the Enclosure Acts, most of which were passed between 1720 and 1840 causing rural poverty and civil unrest. As this popular protest song pithily puts it:

The law locks up the man or woman
Who steals the goose from off the common
But leaves the greater villain loose
Who steals the common from off the goose.

Anonymous, mid-eighteenth century

For the nature poet John Clare (1793–1864) the acts represented the demise of freedom to roam the countryside, a loss that he mourned in a series of poems such as this:

A board sticks up to notice 'no road here'
And on the tree with ivy overhung
The hated sign by vulgar taste is hung
As tho' the very birds should learn to know
When they go there they must no further go

John Clare, 'The Mores', 1812–1831

Today, village greens are all that remain of common grassland in long-established settlements such as Ashley Green and Holmer Green. In my home village the green still hosts the annual village fête, a throwback to the traditional country fair with its coconut shies, tug of war and tombolas. As kids, my brother and I would look forward to the Saturday in June that the fair came to town, when the weather always seemed steamily tropical and the village teenagers would turn out in furtive groups. We'd peruse the stalls and amusements, once winning a forlorn goldfish which we took home in a polythene bag.

I was yet to witness any vestiges of old Holmer Green myself that morning, for I was still walking along the main road towards the modern settlement. Above, at a height of only fifty feet, a red kite orbited the rooftops – my first sighting that day of this Chiltern emblem. When I was growing up here, these majestic birds had long vanished from the hills, yet in the Middle Ages, the red kite was protected by royal decree. Valued as a scavenger that prevented disease by clearing organic waste from our filthy towns and cities, its destruction was a capital offence. Come the 1600s, however, and kites were classed as vermin, hated by gamekeepers and with bounties on their heads. By 1871 they had been driven to extinction in England, followed by Scotland in 1879 – although a handful of breeding pairs managed to cling on in the valleys of deepest Wales. To address the problem, the first Kite Committee was formed as early as 1903, and in the late eighties and early nineties a handful of birds were released at sites in Scotland and the Chilterns. Now, there are estimated to be over a thousand breeding pairs in the Chilterns alone, soaring above almost every landscape.

Even with a kite's eye view, it's hard to fathom today where Hazlemere ends and Holmer Green begins. They share the same solid detached houses, red-brick and tile-roofed (one with a Union Jack hanging limply outside). The same crunchy gravel driveways occupied by shiny SUVs. During my childhood Sundays, driveways such as these streamed with soapy water as the menfolk (and it was always the menfolk), on weekend release from their office jobs, cleaned their cars. No-one appeared to be cleaning cars that Sunday morning: pop-up valeting services can do the job so much better. Instead, the residents of Hazlemere and Holmer Green were spending their Sunday morning clipping their hedges with cordless trimmers.

The air was astringent that day as late summer fused with early autumn. A few months before, when the grass was growing thick and fast, the air would have been heavy with the perfume of cow parsley. That musky scent of early summer and aimless childhood rambles, when all we wished was for the months and years to pass as quickly as possible. To grow older, to grow up. And now that I am grown up, I want to slow it all down. Slow down the springs of country lanes foaming with cow parsley, its creaminess spilling over the verges. Verges which, like the hedges, must now be tamed and strimmed.

The strimmer, or 'string trimmer', was developed in the 1970s by one George Ballas of Texas. A little later in the autumn, when the leaves lie deep on the ground, it's the leaf blower – another American import – that will punctuate Sunday mornings such as these. But in my neck of the beech woods, my father would sweep the wet November foliage into pyramids to burn in our back garden, the melancholy scent filling my nostrils. Our little mound of leaves would smoulder long into the school week, its aroma a reminder of our weekend freedoms. You don't see bonfires in gardens much anymore. The chainsaw, the strimmer and the leaf blower have replaced the scythe, the hoe and the pitchfork as the agricultural tools of the contemporary suburban countryman.

I had nearly given up on finding the village centre, but then, almost hidden by its surrounding ribbon development, I stumbled upon the 'green' in Holmer Green. The Common is a proud, triangular space, its original size reduced by the gracious Victorian villas that surround it today. A homely pub with hipped roof and brick dressings fronts the green, its only nod to the modern world the sign outside reading 'PREMISES UNDER CCTV SURVEILLANCE'. Opposite the pub are the village hall and Victorian church, with the junior school down the road.

This is just the arrangement in my home village: the knapped-flint church by the respected Victorian architect G E Street, a low-beamed pub (the former village smithy) and a village hall. Ours is a 1960s replacement of the hall built by the RAF after World War I in memory of villagers who lost their lives, and for the use of ex-servicemen. Today, I remember it chiefly as the backdrop to village discos, where we'd get tipsy on Party 7 beer and dance to the latest glam rock hits.

Holmer Green still has its village school, but my old Church of England primary school, whose scent of polished floors and school dinners I will never forget, is long closed. It was founded in 1853 by the local bigwigs, a pretty building of russet brick with lozenge-leaded windows, whitewashed bargeboards and gabled roofs. In the surrounding playground, we used to drink our child-sized bottles of milk each break time, warm and slightly sour from being left out in the sun. The teachers were a Mr Jones (the headmaster), a Mrs Jones (the deputy headmistress) and a Miss Jones (who taught the smallest children). They were not related. It was Miss Jones who took us out to pick elderflowers from the hedgerows in Two Dells Lane and taught us beautiful Italic handwriting. Our small fingers, black with Quink, clasped a wide nib to form elegant calligraphy, the original script of Renaissance Italy. Right hand held firm and stiff, so that the nib stayed horizontal to form the wide and narrow strokes of the letters. It must be two decades since I last used a pen to write anything longer than a shopping list or my signature, and my calligraphy skills have long rusted away.

Gone, too, are the incumbent vicar and the resident policeman, the latter once administering an avuncular ticking-off when I was caught riding helmetless on the back of a village boy's moped. But the primary school is now the community centre where pilates, yoga, art and bridge classes are held. Thriving school or demoted community centre – village England is alive and kicking in settlements such as Holmer and Ashley Green.

Antique landscapes such as the one I was walking through that day are palimpsests, layers of history, one lying just beneath another. Sometimes an upper layer peels away, and a buried one is revealed. Such is Kingstreet, which according to my 1880s map existed when Stevenson was here and which leads north from Holmer Green. This was an important drovers' road, where cattle and sheep would be driven across the Chilterns to seasonal fairs and markets. Nowadays its importance is much reduced, there not being much call for drovers anymore. Yet there are still references to the village's connection with drovers and their animals in the street names. I was standing in Penfold Lane (where sheep were penned), having just passed Sheepcote Dell Road. Even the neat bungalows lining the street out of the village still cling on to the old rural traditions, with their allotment gardens and signs advertising home-grown runner beans. And names such as Orchard End hark back to Holmer Green's vanished agricultural past when the village's proximity to London encouraged fruit-growing, its plentiful cherry orchards still studding my 1880s map.

Kingstreet survives today as a bridleway, its entrance hidden at the edge of the village. Too hidden, it seems, as I could not locate it. I paused to check my map, and an elderly couple with labradors approached. They looked very like my parents – he tall, with a cloth cap and gilet, she with a trim grey bob and a smiley face.

'You look like you're on a long-distance walk,' the woman said, touching my arm. I wondered if this was a polite way of informing me that I didn't quite fit in with the Sunday strollers of Holmer Green, with my scruffy hiking gear and old rucksack. Just as the apparently civil enquiry 'can I help you?', when uttered by a certain breed of English person, really means 'what do you think you are you doing here?'

'I *am* on a long-distance walk – to Tring,' I responded to her gentle tease. 'I'm looking for Kingstreet, which goes to Little Missenden.' She pointed me in the right direction.

'It's a bit muddy down there,' she warned as they bade me farewell. Muddier still when it was a drovers' road with flocks of sheep on their own long-distance walk across the Chilterns, I thought as I proffered my thanks.

The end-of-speed-limit sign announced at last the end of High Wycombe, its suburbs, and pleasant, leafy Holmer Green. Then, for the first time that day, abruptly and miraculously, the sun peered from between the clouds, butter-light skimming the beech-tops. And alongside a russet-brick cottage the sign I'd been looking for: Public Bridleway – the entrance to Kingstreet, and its peeling layers of muddy history.

> Bidding good-morning to my fellow-traveller, I left the road and struck across country. It was rather a revelation to pass from between the hedgerows and find quite a bustle on the other side, a great coming and going of school-children upon by-paths, and, in every second field, lusty horses and stout country-folk a-ploughing.

I too, having bid good morning to my fellow travellers, left the road and struck across country. Perhaps I shared with Stevenson his sense of freedom and elation as I left the tarmac for the first time that day. 'Lusty horses' had also trod my bridleway fairly recently, as the hoof-prints beneath my feet bore witness. But these horses would not have been a-ploughing; instead, they would have been bearing their owners on a leisurely Sunday morning hack, the Chilterns being prime horse-riding country. This I remember from my own teenage years growing up here. As schoolgirls we were all horse mad, posters of horses vying with portraits of David Cassidy or Donny Osmond on our bedroom walls (you liked either David or Donny, never both).

On Kingstreet the road noise receded and silence wrapped round me like a mantle. After fifty metres or so I now entered, for the first time on this walk, a world of tranquillity and calm. Birdsong beckoned from the distant woodlands. Remembering Stevenson, I listened out for the 'wonderful carolling of larks' which accompanied him the entire journey. Like him I was walking in autumn, when their celebrated song is less likely to be heard than in spring or summer. But Stevenson did hear them in autumn. Indeed, 'the air was alive with them from High Wycombe to Tring' so I should have heard at least one skylark – even granted their drastic decline in recent decades.

Odes have been written about them, music has been composed for them. Percy Shelley's 'To a Skylark' and Vaughan Williams' *The Lark Ascending* remain some of the most popular works in English culture. At the end of the nineteenth century Flora Thompson noted the 'great number of skylarks' around her Oxfordshire home of Juniper Hill, and named one of the best-loved books about rural England after them. But by the time that *Lark Rise to Candleford* was published in 1945, skylarks were already in decline. During most of the nineteenth century they were popular as caged songbirds and sold for food in the markets of Britain and Europe. The author Simon Holloway, in *The Historical Atlas of Breeding Birds in Britain and Ireland 1875–1900*, estimates that in 1854, twenty years before Stevenson walked the Chilterns, 400,000 skylarks were sold in London markets alone. They were mainly caught by dragnet, torn from their groundcover in much same way that modern trawlers dredge the ocean floor. By the end of the century the fashion for eating skylarks had died out, and the birds had a brief respite until after World War II when intensive farming began to take hold. And with it, the freefall in numbers we see today.

Now, in the forty years since I lived in the Chilterns, populations of skylarks have fallen by seventy-five percent. Most of this decline took place between the mid 1970s and the mid 1980s, and although the rate of decline has slowed in the past two decades there are only an estimated 1,500,000 breeding pairs remaining in Britain. Their status is now listed as red-for-danger, meaning they are globally threatened. Planting our cereals in autumn rather than spring has been blamed, the winter wheat so favoured by modern farmers growing denser, taller and harder for the birds to build their nests in. Pesticides and herbicides destroy their food source in arable regions, and in pastoral areas increased grazing has left pasture too short for the birds to nest.

So it was with hope rather than expectation of hearing a skylark that I found myself walking between two tall hedges, still dense with summer foliage and fringed with stinging nettles. The blackberries hung overripe and rotting from their brambles, fruit which Stevenson's 'stout country folk' would have valued to supplement their meagre diet. Growing up we too used to look forward to blackberrying, taking atavistic pleasure in collecting the fat, purple fruit to make blackberry and apple crumble. But there was no-one else on this particular fruit-laden path at all, even though it was a Sunday morning. Stevenson might have found 'quite a bustle' on the other side of the hedgerows, but today all was quiet except for a pair of handsome bay horses, munching the grass. A sign on a five-bar gate read 'PRIVATE KEEP OUT. NO PATH THIS WAY'.

The track widened as the hazel hedges, bent and braided by hand over centuries, gave way to woodland. The Chilterns remains one of the most densely wooded regions in England, with an estimated one quarter of its area covered in trees. As my 1880s map confirmed, this particular stretch, Coleman's Wood and Haleacre Wood, is exactly the size and shape now as it was in Stevenson's time and conceals the remains of a moated site where medieval pottery has been excavated. This ditched enclosure, one of around six thousand known in England, is the medieval manor house of Holmer. I made a feeble attempt to look for the earthworks, but was turned back by wire fencing and another 'PRIVATE PLEASE KEEP OUT' sign (at least there was a 'please' this time). The *cole* in Coleman's Wood, historians believe, probably refers to the charcoal makers who would have managed these woods for fuel before the industrial extraction of coal from mines. Woods were working places once, not the countrified amenities for walkers and horse riders that they are today.

Wider still the track, and greater still the sense of walking on an ancient thoroughfare. Descending steeply, Kingstreet sinks into the earth from centuries of footfall. A sudden clearing, a breach in the hedge and I looked down, over a stubble plain, to a scene – a mirage, almost – of village England. Little Missenden lay cocooned in the Misbourne Valley, its flint church tower winking in the autumn sunshine. Beyond, the hillside rose steeply from the valley bottom, its upper slopes clad with beech hangars.

Hangar: 'wood on steep side of hill';
from Old English *hangra*, 'hang'

Geologists have a term for this characteristic Chiltern topography in which the land has eroded more dramatically on one side of the valley (usually south and west facing) than the other. They call them 'asymmetric dry valleys', with the gentler northern slopes, such as where I now stood, being more suited to cultivation. But even the arid language of geologists could not detract from the tableau before me that day. In the foreground, the village cricket team was playing perhaps its last game of summer. Ripples of applause wafted up from the vale as a run was made or a catch taken, and mingled with the birdsong in the tree canopy above. If you could ignore the pylons striding gigantically across the hillside, little appeared changed since Stevenson travelled here.

I turned back from this dream of Middle England, a microcosm of old certainties in an uncertain world, and continued down the deeply hollowing holloway. Twisted beech roots, like arthritic fingers, emerged from earth banks almost as tall as me. The trees leaned in, branches interlacing over my head like clasping hands.

Above the treetops the early autumn sun was warm, but the air beneath was cool and damp. I was lured further into this verdant tunnel by birdsong, sucked deeper and darker into England's rural past on a venerable road once trod by drovers and tradesmen, churchgoers and soldiers, merchants and missionaries.

The track emerged at a crossroad, marked by a discarded Bulmer's Cider bottle. This track was the first official long-distance path of my journey: the South Bucks Way. I looked back, and my holloway was lost now, hidden behind its leafy portal. The path edged around the stubble plain, and sheep – a rare sight in the Chilterns nowadays – grazed the pasture. 'LITTLE MISSENDEN WELCOMES CAREFUL DRIVERS,' a sign declared as I entered the village. 'SLOW! CHILDREN AND HORSES CROSSING,' advised another. I paused for a few minutes at the Little Missenden Misfits Cricket Club, its entrance marked by a stately old oak tree, to see close-up the game that had so enchanted me from the hillside. On the veranda of the pavilion batsmen waited their turn, the younger members of the team slumped over their smartphones. Warmed by the sun, the pavilion exhaled the acrid scent of creosote. Along with musky cow parsley, this was the fragrance of a Chiltern childhood and memories of summers past.

The summer of 1976, one of the hottest in living memory. I was supposed to be swotting for exams, but my books lay open on the ground and Radio One crackled from the transistor.

The tar bubbled on the roads; trickles of sweat ran down the back of my neck. Green-check dress, frumpy school issue, stuck to my skin. Our school teachers, usually so stiff and buttoned up, removed their tights – or, the racy thought seeped into our fevered minds, were they stockings? – and bared their legs, scandalously. After school each afternoon I stretched out with my revision on the lawn, with its deep brown patches where our golden retriever had peed. From beyond the hedge the provincial purr of a lawn mower chewed the edges of my consciousness. A faint shiver ruffled the sun-bleached hairs on my arms as dusk fell. I folded the deckchairs and returned them to the garden shed, the smell of creosote pricking my nostrils.

Leaving the Little Missenden Misfits to their games of cricket and Pokémon Go, I headed towards the village centre. Stevenson provides very little topographical detail of his walk so I don't know if he passed this precise way. But if he didn't, he would have missed one of the indisputable gems of the Chilterns.

The mirage viewed from the hilltop did not dissolve as I drew near, as desert oases are fabled to do on the approach of thirsty travellers. Close-up it's still a vision of village England. Weather-boarded barns are now fine residences hidden behind electronically operated gates. Ruddy brick cottages with tiled roofs and bulging bow windows – no longer the humble homes of *cottars*, or farm labourers – fringe the village green. Wisteria frames doorways, verges are neatly mown. Parked outside, Range Rovers have replaced the haywains. You can quite see why stressed-out city folk and tired retirees want to retreat into this dream of an unchanging England. The careful tending of flowers, the mowing of lawns, the trimming of hedges is a barricade against external forces they can no longer control: forces such as HS2.

A chime of bells from the tower of St John the Baptist summoned, and I sat down in its timber-framed porch to eat my lunch. Notices warned that the roof was alarmed, just in case you were lulled into forgetting that this was the twenty-first century when church roofs are routinely stripped for their lead. Inside, medieval paintings – painstakingly conserved with the help of Lottery funding to the tune of £305,000 – cover much of the walls, a remarkable survival of both the Puritans who whitewashed such idolatry and the Victorian penchant for stripping church interiors of their plasterwork.

As I admired a particularly fine representation of St Christopher, along with that familiar churchy scent of damp plaster, polished wood and candlewax, the vicar strode in. Bald, tanned and smiling, he bade me hello. He looked happy in his work and I couldn't blame him – I could imagine a no more agreeable parish in which to shepherd one's flock. Alive and well in Little Missenden was the comfortable, comforting Chiltern tribe I had left behind so many decades ago.

I finished my shrink-wrapped ploughman's sandwich, bought that morning at High Wycombe station, although I didn't think it had ever been within sniffing distance of a ploughman. Outside, a vapour of drizzle descended and a well turned-out gentleman appeared from the doorway, carrying chairs and tables into the churchyard. 'They're for the cream teas they serve every Sunday afternoon in fine weather,' he said, as I pulled a waterproof out of my rucksack. It was early autumn, the rain was falling, yet the stoic optimism of a Chiltern summer lingered on.

> The lanes were profoundly still. They would have been sad but for the sunshine and the singing of the larks. And as it was, there came over me at times a feeling of isolation that was not disagreeable, and yet was enough to make me quicken my steps eagerly when I saw someone before me on the road.

The lanes were profoundly still that Sunday afternoon too, although sadly no larks were singing. My feeling of isolation was not disagreeable either, as I followed in the footsteps of Stevenson's lovesick ghost. Heading away from Little Missenden along a narrow road marked on my map as Chalk Lane, the idyll was ruptured by the grumble from the A413 which now bypasses the village. Stevenson, the scion of a great engineering dynasty, might have approved of this road, but I did not as I scurried across, dodging the traffic.

Chalk Lane now led me out of the Misbourne Valley and up into the chalk uplands, and once again I became aware of the geological and climatic forces that shaped these hills. From around 145 million years ago the Chiltern chalk started to form under sub-tropical seas, to be thrust upwards by massive tectonic forces some eighty million years later. And although they were never entirely covered by glaciers during the Ice Ages, their tundra-like hills were carved by ice and frost to emerge as vertebrae in a spine of chalk hills that run from the Dorset Downs in southern England to the Yorkshire Wolds in the north.

It is the Chilterns that John Bunyan is thought to be describing when he writes in *The Pilgrim's Progress* (1678) of 'a most Pleasant Mountainous Country, beautified with Woods, Vineyards, Fruits of all sorts; Flowers also with Springs and Fountains, very delectable to behold'. Three hundred and forty years on and Chiltern woodlands are beautiful yet: fruit and flowers still grow in Chiltern gardens and vineyards still prosper on their slopes. Looking back from the top of just such a slope I could no longer see Little Missenden, sequestered in its valley. This mirage of village England had dissolved back into the miasma from where it came.

As I passed under the railway bridge a train rumbled overhead. Turning left into a spinney I walked alongside the track for a while, brushed by blackthorn heavy with sloes. Such hedgerows were planted to keep animals off the line when it opened in the late nineteenth century: a swathe of nature is destroyed by a train, another thrives in its place.

Spinney: 'a small copse or wood; from Latin *spīna*, 'thorn', Middle English *spenné*

This peaceful blackthorn spinney led to Mantle's Wood, another tract of ancient woodland. Hazel and hornbeam, ash and beech grow in Mantle's Wood, the habitat providing a home to the delicate rare moschatel flower and colonies of pipistrelle bats.

HS2 was scheduled to slice through here, felling trees up to thirty metres each side of the cutting for 'vegetation management', before campaigners persuaded HS2 Ltd to tunnel under the wood instead. One small victory for this sliver of Chiltern landscape in a war of overwhelming odds.

From across the valley the sound of guns ricocheted through the treetops, the 'dropping fire' of gunshot also heard by Stevenson almost 150 years previously. The birds had now fallen silent. Perhaps, like the residents of South Heath, they too had sold up and left, fearful for the future of this stately old wood. The sun was warm as I now entered open fields, the old season tussling with the new like mature and youthful bucks sparring for dominance. For now, the old buck was still the stronger, and they'd be serving those cream teas down in Little Missenden after all.

The path led through a stubble field, the first shoots of winter wheat poking up through umber earth. In a few months' time this field would take on the acid-green of spring when, after a winter of lying dormant, the wheat would quiver in spray-deadened ground. Then would come the scorched gold of high summer, when the grain crackles in the hot June wind like paper and the acrid taste of glyphosate – sprayed on crops to accelerate the drying process – fills the mouth.

But for now, in autumn shades of tan and taupe, flints glinting white in slanting sun, the earth lay dormant, soft and silent. I was walking high in an English field, chasing the cloud shadows as they rolled across the hills ahead, my boots scrunching on flinty soil. But still no skylarks sang.

Across the field a couple of fellow walkers sat, eating sandwiches. They were up from London for the day, doing a circular hike of the Chilterns having caught the train to Chesham, the final stop on its branch of the Metropolitan Line. The railway of John Betjeman's *Metro-Land*, cutting its swathe through the Chiltern landscape. Modern and shiny once, it is unpretentious now in the face of its brash usurper, HS2. Today, the Chilterns remains the closest AONB to London, and the only one you can get to by Underground.

Alongside the wood the first fallen leaves of autumn fringed the fields, last year's leaves powdering underfoot. The path now entered Hedgemoor Wood. Beech, ash and wild cherry. Hazel, hawthorn and holly. Elder, box and yew. Maple, birch and sycamore. Another ancient woodland spared – for now – by the tunnel that will soon burrow worm-like beneath the earth. This tessellated landscape of woods and fields, meadows and hedge-lined lanes, long-legged horses and weather-boarded barns, village cricket teams and churchyard cream teas, muddy bridleways and saggy roofs, electronically operated gates and PRIVATE KEEP OUTS.

The decision to tunnel under this stretch of the Chilterns came too late for some of the families who, until recently, lived here. Leaving Hedgemoor Wood I crossed Hyde Lane, an old way coiling up from the valley bottom and bisecting this hamlet of listed farmhouses once due to be flattened by HS2. The owners of two of these farmhouses sold up to HS2 Ltd, who were then persuaded to extend the tunnel leaving the houses empty and the heart ripped out of the community. A bittersweet victory for the residents of Hyde Lane, past and present.

Hyde: 'amount of land sufficient to support a household'; from Old English *hȳd*

Across a vast tawny prairie, the old field boundaries and my footpath were now lost under the plough. I ploughed on regardless, towards a hedge forming an impermeable barrier ahead. Up close, a rupture in the foliage revealed otherwise. Not an obstacle, but an aperture opening into a parallel world, like climbing through the wardrobe into Narnia. I was high up on the Chiltern plateau now, all dry stubble and brown earth. I could not see Great Missenden clustered in the valley below, but I could feel it. There was the sense of a walk ending as the day expired, of a destination attained. And, in a long linear walk such as this, if only of three days and twenty miles duration, the sense of a staging post reached.

I don't know if Stevenson walked exactly this route, but he describes being given directions by a 'little old maid' he met along the way:

> She told me, very explicitly, to follow the path until I came to the end of the wood, and then I should see the village below me in the bottom of the valley. And, with mutual courtesies, the little old maid and I went on our respective ways. Nor had she misled me. Great Missenden was close at hand, as she had said, in the trough of a gentle valley, with many great elms about it.

There was no maid on hand to offer me directions, and the 'great many elms' he saw in 1874 were destroyed by Dutch elm disease just a century later.

Dutch elm disease was one of the defining natural events of the 1970s, yet I remember it only hazily growing up. I didn't even know what an English elm looked like, though it figures in the paintings of Constable and Turner, and has been eulogised by poets from John Clare to John Betjeman. Elms in art and literature were a symbol of permanence, part of the unchanging landscape of England. Those poets and painters seem to have drawn solace from the notion that when they themselves were gone from this world these great, ceremonial trees would remain. John Clare, in his poem 'The Fallen Elm', mourned the loss of a single tree. How could they have imagined that all the elms of England would, one day, be gone too?

But the loss of the elms didn't seem a calamity to me then, and only faintly do I remember the news reports on the devastation. Only as I get older do I grieve for the loss of these veterans of the English landscape, these quiet stalwarts that had been growing on our islands for eight thousand years and proved the inspiration for so many. Those 'great many elms' must have offered inspiration to Stevenson too, as he trudged down towards Great Missenden at the end of his day's walk. And like Stevenson's, my first sight of the town was the church, which 'sits well back on its haunches against the hillside', set apart from the heart of a village which seems to have slipped down the hillside. It was this church I was heading for, as I descended steeply through the pillowy landscaped park of Missenden Abbey. The abbey has a long and eventful history. Starting life as Augustinian monastery in 1133, it was dissolved by Henry VIII in 1538 then rebuilt as a private mansion in the fashionable neo-Gothic style. Following a major fire in 1985 it was reincarnated – having risen phoenix-like from the ashes – as a conference centre and wedding venue. But with dusk descending I hurried on past, towards the church instead.

There was a light on inside the Church of St Peter and St Paul when I turned up, and the car park was full. A hum of voices floated from the half-open doors, so I squinted in. 'Cream teas with music, Sundays 3–5pm', a notice by the porch proclaimed. A buzz of conversation and a twang of strings led me inside, where classical guitarists played to a scattered crowd of parishioners sitting in the pews, tea trays balanced on knees. From the tops of the piers, gargoyles peered down from five hundred years ago upon white-haired ladies, who bustled about, hawking home-made jams and pickles with polite insistence. Other white-haired ladies proffered hearty cakes, brooking no refusal. Groups of walkers filed in, cold and tired, and were offered succour in the form of that old British stalwart, a nice cup of tea. One rambler confided, a little sheepishly, that they'd been on a murder mystery walk, Great Missenden being one of the locations for the long-running TV series *Midsomer Murders*. Chiltern communities may be being splintered by modern commuter life, and fractured by HS2, but they are healing themselves on Sunday afternoons in serene village churches such as this.

It was raining again when I tore myself from this pleasant interlude to continue down to the village centre, and the end of my day's journey. The town was just a few minutes' walk away, the old lane undercut by the A413 which since the 1960s has severed the church from its community. The traffic growl faded, and I was walking along a lane of brick cottages and flinty façades to emerge onto the High Street. Opposite, boarded up and forlorn, was the medieval George Inn, all leaning gables and leaded casements. Behind was the manorial courthouse, timber-framed and sagging under its tiled roof. Condemned with the inn to be turned into 'four residential dwellings' until the Save The George campaign group stepped in, it's now been listed as an Asset of Community Value by Chiltern District Council and villagers hope to restore it as an inn once again. Stevenson doesn't tell us if he spent the night at The George – there are plenty of other cosy old inns in Great Missenden – but as I gazed on this old survivor from another age, I rather liked to think he did.

The Historian

The Church of St Peter and St Paul was hushed when I returned the next morning. No trace of the previous day's jollity, not even a stray cake crumb on its worn tiled floor. From the tops of their piers the gargoyles now looked down upon empty pews. It was here that I'd arranged to meet Alison Doggett, a local historian who has spent a lifetime studying the landscape of her Chiltern homeland.

Alison is a retired geography teacher, a grandmother and an author. Blonde hair framed her face, and her love of the Chilterns radiated with the passion of youth. She had brought with her an armful of documents which she unfurled over a table where, the previous afternoon, cream teas were served. Taking out my own map I showed her where today's walk would lead me, on paths and lanes high above the Missenden Valley.

'It's very pretty up there,' she said, a note of wistfulness in her voice. It's an area she knows well, having lived until recently in Kings Ash, a hamlet on my intended route along Kings Lane. She had also researched the valley for a paper on market effects of HS2 for the Chilterns AONB Conservation Board.

'It's a fairly dull read, but when I was researching it I remembered this 1620 map and discovered the original in Bucks Historical Record Office. It's as big as a bed-sheet – this is a small version of it.' She smoothed out a still-sizeable photocopy onto the table. 'It has every single field on it, but you can also see the A413, as it's called today.'

'That's the old London to Aylesbury road, isn't it?'

'Yes. When I saw the map I thought – those fields, and the little lanes, have not changed for centuries. So I took a Google Earth image of the field pattern and I put it next to the map, and it's almost identical.' Alison showed me where she had overlaid the modern image above the original map. 'I can't tell you how astounded we were when we found this stuff,' she added.

A stream of sunlight cascaded in through the stained-glass windows, spilling onto the polished table-top where the two maps were spread. She explained that we were looking at a truly historic landscape – one that had barely changed since the Middle Ages. Medieval fields, Alison told me, were based on Anglo-Saxon field patterns so most of them will be a thousand years old. The hedgerows, the boundaries and the lanes are still all exactly the same, and follow the route of the fields.

'The Chilterns didn't farm easily as it's chalky, and the soils are thin and full of flints,' said Alison. She went on to describe how the region was at the very margin of the last Ice Age. The glacier stopped on the edge of the Chiltern Hills, so every summer when it melted the meltwater would pour over the top of the hills and carve the characteristic steep valleys, making the topography much more fragmented than most other chalk areas of England. The result is lots of little dry valleys and wooded hilltops that have remained wooded because they're difficult to farm. A few of the small fields have amalgamated, and some of them that were arable or pasture are now woodland, and vice versa. As someone who'd always assumed that landscape history was one of continual degradation and loss, I could now see that change sometimes reinvigorates the countryside.

Alison pointed down again at the maps. 'You can see that the parishes are arranged perpendicular to the scarp edge, and they're long skinny strips like fingers. When the land was divided up in Anglo-Saxon times everybody got an equitable bit of greensand, clay bottom, a steep bit and some wood on the hills.'

'That's what the Norse settlers did in the Yorkshire Dales, where I live,' I said. 'You get the long strips going up the hillside, and everyone got an equal bit of land.'

'Yes, it's the same thing here, because you needed a bit of everything. You needed your grazing, which was really important, and in the Chilterns you needed your wood.'

But then came the practice of enclosure, whereby common land – fields, meadows and pastures – that had for centuries been communally farmed and grazed was awarded to local landowners by acts of Parliament. Between the early seventeenth and the early nineteenth centuries over five thousand acts of enclosure were passed, covering almost seven million acres of countryside. In the Chilterns, Alison explained, all they did was enclose the edges of some of the fields with hedges, amalgamating them but not changing the basic pattern.

'We still have more hedges than almost anywhere else,' she continued. 'The Chiltern hedges are a study in themselves. A lot of people have walked along them to count the number of species because that's one of the ways of telling how old they are. Some of these hedgerows have been here for thousands of years.'

'And soon they're going forever.' Now it was my turn to feel wistful.

We looked at the map the Conservation Board had made. It showed exactly how HS2 will cut this ancient landscape in half. Alison indicated a slender road running across the top of the plateau.

'This is Kings Lane. When you walk along it later you'll see where the railway line is going to go, because it follows the pylons in the adjoining fields.'

'So the train is going to go overland along this point?'

'Yes, on a huge viaduct. Here, at Hunts Green Farm they're going to have a very big spoil dump, though they've got a fancy name for it. The soil that they're digging up will be piled up in Hunts Green Farm and the farmer's going to lose a great chunk of it for a long time. Eventually he'll get it back, though we're not sure whether he'll be able to continue farming. He'll get some compensation, but it's not the same as losing your farm.'

I scrutinised the map: I would be passing Hunts Green Farm later that day. But Alison had already moved on, pointing to a wood further along the map. 'The line crosses here, at Jones' Hill Wood, this tiny triangle of ancient woodland. When we looked at the 1620 map it was a little triangle then, shaped like a tear. And it hasn't changed. Think of all the years!'

She told me that the Chilterns has large tracts of ancient woodland, with many dating back a thousand years.

'There's a reason why people in this part of the world were particularly distressed about HS2,' she continued. 'Of all the AONB they could go through, they chose the widest part and the highest part. All of this will be naked chalk for a very long time, a huge scar because the chalk is so close to the surface.'

Her words reminded me of the cutting through the chalk on the M40, the Stokenchurch Gap, still there forty years on like an open wound. I pass through it every time I drive from Oxford to London.

'So is there anything left to be done?' I asked. 'I'm quite surprised, because I haven't seen much protest on my walk so far. It's almost as if it wasn't happening.'

'Oh, there's been masses of protests. There are lots of signs, and if you go along the A413 there is knitting on the trees to show where the line will go.'

'I'd love to see that! Where's the knitting?'

'Down on the main road, and where it crosses these ancient lanes like Chesham Lane, Leather Lane, Bowood Lane – all adorable. Some of these may be widened to provide access for construction vehicles, and that is heartbreaking because ancient Anglo-Saxon lanes like this are not two-a-penny.' She pulled out a photograph of Bowood Lane, taken in summer when the rosebay willowherb was in bloom. 'Can you see how it curves round before it goes down? That's because the strip fields finished on this lane, so that you could have access to your strip.

Bowood Lane is delicious – it still has grass growing up the middle.'

'That's my favourite sort of lane, too,' I agreed.

'Where these lanes meet the main road, there's knitting. People have knitted great long scarves, all in different colours. They tie the scarves to the trees.'

I was reminded, once again, of the Newbury bypass protesters chaining themselves to trees in the 1990s. Guerrilla knitting seemed a far more picturesque and civilised way to go about it.

The morning was advancing, and I'd still got a whole day's walk ahead. We took a last look at the old map.

'The other interesting thing about this map is that it was commissioned by a woman,' Alison said. The woman was Dame Mary Wolley, and she inherited the estates of Wendover and Wendover Forrens – along with the Chequers Estate – on her marriage. Her portrait still hangs in Chequers Great Hall.

'The marriage was arranged by her grandfather and it wasn't a happy one, which is hardly surprising if you marry a ten-year-old when you're twelve,' Alison continued. 'But when she was in her thirties she got this chap called Henry Lily, who was a fantastic mapmaker, to draw detailed maps of her estate. So Dame Mary did one really good thing in her life.'

We began to gather up our things ready to leave: Alison the copies of her old maps, me my rucksack. After an hour of conversation, Alison's zeal for her subject had not waned.

'I liken it to the fairytale of the Princess and the Pea,' she concluded. 'Like the mattresses in the story, you're peeling back the landscape. We've got to 1620, though it goes back much further because this is a relic of a landscape that was developed a thousand years ago.'

Alison and I left the church to walk back down to the village, where she had parked her car and where the second day of my walk was to begin. Dame Mary Wolley, the women serving teas in the church the previous day, the guerrilla knitters and Alison Doggett with her erudition and enthusiasm. Spirited women standing up for their convictions in their civilised, Home Counties way. All of them knitted together into the fabric of Middle England like woollen strands in those scarves wrapped around the trees on the A413 road between London and Aylesbury.

DAY TWO

Great Missenden
to
Wendover

> Wendover ... lies in the same valley with Great Missenden, but at the foot of it, where the hills trend off on either hand like a coast-line, and a great hemisphere of plain lies, like a sea, before one, I went up a chalky road, until I had a good outlook over the place. The vale, as it opened out into the plain, was shallow, and a little bare, perhaps, but full of graceful convolutions.

Missenden: 'valley where marsh plants grow'; from Old English *Myssedene*

My walk back from St Peter and St Paul took me along Church Street and its rows of former artisans' cottages, built of brick and flint. You could quite imagine foul deeds taking place behind those alluring closed doors, in crime fiction if not in real life. There was a sense of something dark lingering behind these Instagrammable façades, this smokescreen of English village perfection.

Perhaps that's why Roald Dahl lived in Great Missenden so long, writing stories of 'black savagery' in his garden shed, his legs wrapped in an old sleeping bag. His writing hut is a replica of Dylan Thomas's, perched high on its Carmarthenshire cliff, which Dahl visited and admired. Dahl's own early life was one of loneliness, loss and violence, concluding with a crash-landing in the Libyan desert as a young World War II fighter pilot. Was the tranquillity of an English country garden just what he needed to create the macabre, darkly comic stories for which he is best known? After thirty-six years in Great Missenden Roald Dahl died here in 1990, his simple gravestone a site of modern pilgrimage amid the quietude of the churchyard of St Peter and St Paul.

Robert Louis Stevenson and Roald Dahl were not the only authors drawn to the Chilterns. The poet Rupert Brooke walked these hills before World War I prematurely ended his life, travelling to Wendover by train and writing a poem in their praise:

I shall desire and I shall find
The best of my desires;
The autumn road, the mellow wind
That soothes the darkening shires.
And laughter, and inn-fires.

White mist about the black hedgerows,
The slumbering Midland plain,
The silence where the clover grows,
And the dead leaves in the lane,
Certainly, these remain.

Rupert Brooke, 'The Chilterns', *Collected Poems*, 1916

Just ten miles down the A413, in Chalfont St Giles, lived the poet John Milton (1608–74) who chose this once-secluded village to escape the plague then ravaging the country, dictating his masterpiece *Paradise Lost* in a rustic cottage in the village centre. You can still visit Milton's house, and the garden that perhaps inspired his description of Eden:

Laurel and Myrtle and what higher grew
Of firm and fragrant leaf: on either side
Acanthus, and each odourous bushy shrub
Fenc'd up the verdant wall, each beauteous flower,
Iris all hues, Roses and Jessamine
Reard high their flourish'd heads between, and wrought
Mosaic.

John Milton, *Paradise Lost*, Book 4

But there was another author on my mind as I left Great Missenden that fresh autumn morning. Dodging the lorries, I dashed across the A413 – originally built as a turnpike road in the mid eighteenth century – to look for the old path up and out of the valley. Could this be the 'chalky road' Robert Louis Stevenson describes climbing to gain 'a good outlook over the place'? I couldn't be sure, but I was pretty certain that this ancient track would shortly become the haul road for access to HS2's tunnel portal at the top of the hill. This soothing meadow, rising towards its hilltop beech wood, would soon be rumbling with construction traffic seven days a week, for up to five years, and carrying an estimated 451 vehicles a day.

But this morning all was serenity as the sun warmed the grass, and the warmed grass smelled of summer still. Stevenson described the day he left Great Missenden as 'sunny overhead and damp underfoot, with a thrill in the air like a reminiscence of frost'. Today, summer was winning the tussle of the seasons. The nettles still stung my hands as I brushed past them, the flies still buzzed about my head. There was even a grasshopper whirring near my feet. If I was to hear a lark on my walk, this was the day I was going to hear it. Though any lark singing in this meadow would have had to compete with the whine of a jet overhead as it descended towards Heathrow Airport, twenty-five miles away.

Just before entering Stockings Wood I turned around to look back at Great Missenden huddled in the valley below, safe in its beechy embrace. The shouts of schoolchildren floated up from the village, fusing with the fading moan of traffic. A metal swing gate giving access to the wood was dedicated to 'Heather K Herrington, 1941–2008, who led so many walks in the Chilterns'. Part of the Chiltern Society's 'donate a gate' scheme to open up access to the countryside by replacing difficult-to-climb stiles, it was another example of this community coming together for the greater good. Heather Herrington's legacy endured as I crossed the threshold into Stockings Wood.

A fallen beech tree lay across the path, its roots still grasping the chalk they'd wrenched from the ground. Beeches, with their spreading roots, are well suited to this chalky bedrock and shallow topsoil, but are still vulnerable to strong winds.

Some 1.75 million beeches were lost in the great October storm of 1987. The unseasonably mild weather meant that most trees were still in leaf, resisting the wind like sails on a ship. Unlike ships, however, the trees had nowhere to go so they toppled to the ground like felled soldiers. Stockings Wood was evidently spared. According to my Ordnance Survey map, it has survived in exactly the same size and shape as when Stevenson walked these hills. And if the 1620 map of the Misbourne Valley unearthed by Alison Doggett is accurate, probably for very much longer.

Stocking: 'a clearing'; from Old English *stocc*, 'stump', Old Norse *stokkr* 'tree-trunk'

Stockings Wood is one of the lucky survivors. Woods like these are being lost all over England to road building, housing and – in the Chilterns – to HS2. They have formed the backdrop to my own life, their leaf mould the musty odour of reluctant Sunday morning walks with my family. Woods such as the Hockeridges, near our home in Ashley Green, are old too, though many of the mature native trees were felled in the 1930s and 1940s to help the war effort. In 1952 the wood was rescued by Mary Wellesley, great-great-granddaughter of the Duke of Wellington, and replanted with ornamental forest trees. Now, pine from Corsica, spruce from Norway and snake-bark maple from China grow alongside native species. Like most Chiltern woodland it was once worked for timber. It still is – though with modern tractors and logging vehicles now replacing the bodgers and charcoal workers. It is currently, according to the information boards scattered amongst its trees, also managed as an 'amenity'.

Amenity: 'a desirable or useful feature or facility'; from Latin *amoenitas* 'pleasant place'

'Amenity' may be an archaic word but its use is thoroughly contemporary, revealing that modern division between work and leisure. The compartmentalisation of life that perhaps didn't manifest itself so starkly when Stevenson walked these hills and people and place were profoundly intertwined.

The intensively managed Hockeridge Woods of my childhood now feel rather alien. Give me instead the secretive unkempt beech wood where I was walking now, overlooking the serene Misbourne Valley. And together with the beech, give me horse chestnuts whose glossy brown conkers littered the ground beneath my boots. Conkers, those marvellous natural jewels of childhood, their velvety crowns and fresh sheen so full of promise. We'd collect them from the ground, or throw sticks to knock them from their branches, prising open their prickly green shells to claim the treasures inside, like pearls from an oyster. My younger brother and his friends would pickle theirs in vinegar to harden the skins, drilling holes for string to use in knuckle-rapping conker fights. I preferred mine fresh and unsullied, yet within a day or two the lustre had faded, the skins had shrivelled and I'd throw the conkers away, disappointed. An early lesson in the transience of youth, and of life itself.

Now, on the other side of Stockings Wood, all sound from the valley had vanished. Climbing still, I passed the vestige of an old apple orchard in a corner of the meadow, dropping its fruit uneaten to the earth. Ashley Green was also once surrounded by orchards. An aerial photo taken in 1928 shows the village encased by groves of apple, plum and cherry. Ashley Green's orchards were once nationally famed, attracting seasonal pickers who set up camp every summer at the so-called 'Wooden Babylon' on the village outskirts. One nurseryman, a Mr Lane, grew a variety of cooking apple called Lane's Prince Albert, named with the permission of Queen Victoria whose pheasants he also supplied. Since the late 1940s, when many newcomers settled in Ashley Green, these orchards have been grubbed up and replaced with houses that nod to their former existence in names such as 'Codlins' (an old variety of cooking apple) and 'Orchard Leigh'. There used to be seventy acres of orchards in the fields along our lane. They were cleared when Britain joined what used to be called the Common Market as the apples were of mixed variety and not of high enough quality. My mother claims that apples still fall from a lone survivor of this orchard in their lane each summer. Nobody bothers to collect them, so they lie rotting on the verge.

And then, just as I found myself lulled into reveries of this meadow's history, I was brought up short by a sign barring my way. Ahead, where the portal of HS2 will emerge from under the Chilterns, 'essential maintenance' to the electricity pylons was taking place and I was forbidden to take another step. The shouts of workmen scaling the pylon in front of me confirmed the warning.

I had no choice but to turn back and retrace my steps to the bottom of the hill and walk up the busy main road to South Heath.

South Heath is a prosperous community, and one that will bear much of the brunt of HS2. Having failed to get the tunnel extended under the whole of the AONB, the inhabitants will see the railway emerging from a portal just north of the village. If the tunnel had been extended another six miles, to beyond Wendover, then it would have emerged outside the AONB. As it is, the tunnel will descend under the River Misbourne – twice – then climb uphill in one of the steepest gradients in the whole of Network Rail, to surface near the top of one of the most historic and unspoiled valleys in the entire Chilterns.

Now, walking into the village, I was entering the eye of the storm, the illusory calm before the maelstrom of HS2. It was a Monday morning, but an unnatural hush settled over the village like the first autumn mists. My 1880s map shows little development where modern South Heath is, only Sibley's Coppice, another ancient woodland of oak and beech wood scattered with rowan, cherry and birch. Coppices are woodland in which the trees or shrubs are periodically cut back to ground level to stimulate growth and provide firewood or timber, the woodland being managed sustainably to provide fuel for generations of villagers.

Coppice: from Old French *copeiz*; originally from medieval Latin *colpus* 'a blow'

Sibley's Coppice was to be partially destroyed by the construction of the railway before campaigners won a reprieve, persuading HS2 Ltd to extend the tunnel to just beyond the village centre. Leaving the coppice behind I walked away from the modern village and towards the historic heart of the community. This stretch of ancient Kings Lane is known as Potter Row – a throwback to when, thanks to the drift deposits on the Chiltern plateau which contain large amounts of clay, the area was home to a thriving pottery industry.

The Buckinghamshire Archaeological Society has dated the pottery industry here to the thirteenth century. In 1311 the road was known as Le Pottererewe, becoming Pottersrowe in 1509, though pot fragments, such as those found at Bury Farm, date production back some three thousand years.

The medieval pot-making industry might have waned by the time that Stevenson visited the Chilterns, but cottage industries still thrived in Potter Row: while men worked in the fields, the womenfolk plaited the straw grown in surrounding fields for the hat-making industry in nearby Chesham. The 1870s saw a decline in this important supplement to the family income, with competition from cheaper Chinese imports drastically reducing Chiltern family incomes. The Chesham census of 1881 – taken at around the same time as my old map and Stevenson's walk – lists many local occupations that seem quaint to us now: as well as the straw plaiters there were bonnet sewers, shoe riveters, journeyman bakers, dressmakers, pageboys, ploughboys, scholars. Other local people were gainfully employed in jobs that we would still recognise today: farmers, builders, bricklayers, painters, joiners, carpenters.

Walking along Potter Row that day it was hard to imagine the thrum of industry that would once have accompanied my journey along the lane. Villagers and archaeologists have found medieval pot-sherds and waste from kilns scattered among the cottage gardens. The brick-and-flint cottages, built from the clay and stones of the local fields by the villagers themselves, have been spruced up to house modern commuters and retirees. In 1913 many were bought up by the Liberty family, best-known for the department store on London's Regent Street, who then rented them back to farm labourers working on their estate. The Liberty family, descendants of Sir Arthur Lasenby Liberty of nearby Chesham who founded the store in 1875, still own much of the land around here, though they sold their flagship store in 2009.

According to one former local resident, farm labourers once worked the Liberty fields from dawn to dusk, seven days a week, with little more than a barrel of beer and a cheese sandwich to sustain them. Today, roses frame the doorways of twenty-first-century Potter Row and the villagers work their allotments instead, growing vegetables in neat plots opposite their cottages. There was the impression of discreet prosperity in the trimmed hedges and shiny cars. There was no sense that within a few months the peace would be ruptured by construction of a cutting just 250 metres from this quiet lane, and within a few years by up to eighteen trains an hour travelling at 250 miles per hour – faster than any current operating speed in Europe – from early morning to midnight seven days a week.

Looking closely, though, you might have glimpsed an inkling of impending calamity on the day I passed through. 'For Sale' signs were mounted on several mown verges, although many of the properties had already been bought up by HS2 Ltd. Others were still selling on the open market, but at suppressed prices. But more than this there was the sense of a dying community, of everyone having just abandoned their pretty cottages and orderly allotments, leaving them as deserted as the *Mary Celeste*. I longed to find someone to talk to about what was happening here, but it was Monday lunchtime and no-one was around. For the countryside here is not the living, working place it once was. The grand old farmhouses, all timber framing, hipped roofs and massive chimney stacks, are now executive homes with gyms and swimming pools, locked behind their fortress-style gates. There was not even anyone tending the plentiful allotments, now ripe for harvest.

In 1970s Ashley Green there were still a few working farms whose inhabitants tilled the land of their ancestors. You can see them scattered around the parish map: Snowhill Farm (which gave its name to the Snowhill Cottages council estate opposite), Hockeridge Farm and Grove Farm – all named after the topographical features of the landscape which they inhabit. Today there are even fewer working farms, with many of those shown on the parish map now farms in name only.

I now passed Leather Lane, one of those 'adorable' ancient roads so loved by Alison Doggett that curl down through the medieval open fields to the valley below. If all goes according to HS2's plan, this one will soon be, in HS2 parlance, 'permanently realigned'

with a new bridge built over the track. At least it will not, as Alison Doggett first feared, be widened and straightened to create the access haul road. This road will now lead directly up from Great Missenden, through the fields I walked across earlier that morning. I ached to walk down Leather Lane, to feel its stately old hedgerows enclose me and its trees fold over my head. But it too was blocked off due to works on the pylons in the fields below. Pylons which will mark the route of HS2, it apparently being easier to build along existing infrastructure where land ownership has already been documented.

Kings Lane has hedgerows too, and noble old sycamore trees marched along both sides like Roman legionaries. For the first time today, as the lane narrowed and meandered, I was free from the rumble of traffic. Wind and rooks were my companions now, and the high keening kites above. I paused for a moment, leaning over a rickety five-bar gate set between a pair of oak trees, and gazed across the meadow to the valley below. Just a field away from where I was standing, 400-metre-long trains, each carrying 550 passengers, would soon be pounding through every 3.3 minutes. Would anyone be able to hear the kites and the rooks and the wind then?

Leaving the village, and passing a few scattered farms, I had given up hope of finding someone to talk to. The last farmhouse before the turn from Potter Row into Kings Lane was not like the others. It had a threadbare, slightly dishevelled air, all chequered brickwork and bulging tiled roofs. An old plastic chair stood alone in the overgrown garden. It was the first farmhouse I'd seen on my walk that looked like it might actually have a real farmer living in it.

Looking over the wooden gate, I was transported back forty years and walking with my mother to the farm in Johns Lane, Ashley Green, where we used to buy our eggs. Even then this mellow-brick farmstead was one of the last old-fashioned mixed farms left in the parish, run by three successive generations of the same family and eventually taken over by their apple-cheeked daughter. We watched the cows being milked in the old weather-boarded barns, and adopted one of the feral cats that followed us home one day to become a much cherished pet. In the 1970s Johns Lane Farm still looked – and smelled – like a traditional village farmyard. Cow dung, warm straw and silage.

This mingling of old and new – commuters like my father and farmers like these – is pretty much how I remember my village. Not too long ago Ashley Green supported nine working farms. Johns Lane Farm was the last survival, but like so many others around the country it suffered from the low prices paid by the supermarkets for milk. When, in 2012, prices fell below what the family needed to keep their dairy business going they auctioned off their herd, and so the village's last dairy farm ceased operating. They now rent out their grazing land and run a farm shop to supplement their income, with plans to create a community-owned solar energy farm on their land. At least the same family are still occupying the farmhouse, still living a semi-agricultural life. Another dairy farm on the main road through my village, which once used to deliver milk by horse and cart, was not so lucky and was recently advertised for sale as a private residence with an estimated value of around a million pounds.

There was a faded sign on the farmhouse wall in front of me: Hunts Green Farm. This must be the one Alison mentioned. As I stared over the gate into the farmyard, a man with greying curly hair stepped out from the doorway, shaking a mat. Taking my chance, I asked him if he lived there, and would he mind talking to me? Yes, he said, he did live in the farm and yes, he had a few minutes to spare as he couldn't work that day due to the pylon repairs in his fields. He introduced himself as Robert Brown and I asked him how long he'd been living there.

'Three generations; I'm the third.'

'So where did your family come from originally?'

'My father came from Cobblers Hill, which is just on the other side of the valley. He started off engineering, doing farm machinery, and then he came onto the farm with his father and two brothers, and then I've come on since then.'

'And your family before that?'

'They've always been in this area. My mother's family come from Wycombe way,' he replied. 'My mother's mother, her parents were the Lord Mayor and Mayoress of High Wycombe.'

'So, what do you farm here?'

'We do grass, grazing sheep in the winter, and I do haymaking through the summer for horse feed. It's a Liberty Farm – that's Liberty's of Regent Street. We're tenant farmers. The Liberty family owns a lot of land around here.'

Now was the time to bite the HS2 bullet. I asked him how he felt about the new railway.

'The long and short of it is, I'm absolutely fed up to the back teeth talking about it. I've been to Parliament twice, the Select Committee, and I went to the House of Lords as well, back in February. We fought our case and we won, but they still say that "we may need your farm, just in case". For tipping all the spoil.'

'Are they going to compensate you, then?' I ventured, my journalist's nosiness coming to the fore.

'Eventually, but we don't know when. I've been to the newspapers, I've been up to London and I've spoken on Radio Oxford, but you're just banging your head against a wall because they're a ruthless lot of people – a nasty, horrible lot they are. They just come, and they tell you what they're going to do with you, and that's it.'

'And what about the AONB that you're in the middle of?'

'Well, it makes no difference to them, does it? It's going right through the middle of an Area of Outstanding Natural Beauty. It's going through the middle of Grim's Dyke, a heritage site which is just down the field on my land. It's only a dip.'

'It's an Iron Age dip! I'd love to see it...'

'They're doing the pylon wires down there. We can't go through those fields at the moment because they're doing the work and it's out of bounds. But if you can come back later when they've finished for the day, I could show you.'

I knew of Grim's Ditch (or Dyke) from my childhood around here, and was keen to see it.

'That would be great, if you've got the time…'

'Well, after about six or six-thirty we're clear to go down there. Maybe if you could pop back then I could show you exactly where the line is coming through.'

We exchanged farewells, until later.

'You're lucky to find me – I'm not normally around this time of day,' said Robert Brown as he turned to go back inside his unrenovated seventeenth-century farmhouse. I agreed. It was indeed a most serendipitous encounter.

Leaving Robert Brown I continued along Kings Lane, which soon veered off left, the main thoroughfare and its traffic continuing right to the villages at the top of the plateau. This was now a single-track road, becoming even narrower, ever more enigmatic as it threaded its way between open fields. Grass burst through crumbling tarmac, nature reclaiming its territory. Through gaps in the hedgerows there were glimpses now of the Misbourne Valley below, a row of marching pylons marking the route of HS2.

> From the level to which I have now attained the fields were exposed before me like a map, and I could see all that bustle of autumn field-work which had been hid from me yesterday behind the hedgerows, or shown to me only for a moment as I followed the footpath.

Stevenson's description of the countryside unfolding before him was so akin to the view from Kings Lane that I could almost feel him striding beside me that afternoon. Yet although hedgerows still fringe the lanes, much else has changed since he walked here. At this time of year almost a century and a half ago, the countryside hummed to the sounds of farm labourers at their 'autumn field-work'. Until the 1870s, and Stevenson's Chiltern adventure, agriculture was booming. Corn prices were good, the clay topsoil fertilised by chalk dug from 'dells', their remains still visible in local fields.

Dell: 'wooded hollow or valley'; from Old English 'small dale', German dialect *Telle*

My own village, Ashley Green, has a Two Dells Lane. It's lined with ancient hedgerow, much of it remnants of old forest. It was along here that Miss Jones, our primary school teacher, would take us to pick the flowers from the elder shrub to make elderflower 'wine', a wholly innocent activity that is probably denied to today's schoolchildren.

There's also a family of Dells buried in Ashley Green's cemetery. One gravestone is dedicated to Jesse Dell, who passed away in 1878, and another to Kathleen Dell, who died in 1978. It is this local family, featuring prominently in the 1881 census, that is said to have given the name to the road. Were the Dells buried in this cemetery (who once also owned the plot of land on which my parents' house was built) named after the valley – or vice versa? People and places, merging through time.

In an agricultural context and in local dialect, a 'dell' means a dry pit, thought to derive from the Old English, *delfan*: to dig, from which the modern word 'delve' originates. The Lollard preacher, John Ball, used this old word when rousing the peasantry in revolt against their feudal masters and famously asking, 'When Adam delved and Eve span, who was then the gentleman?' The rebellion was put down and John Ball was tried and hanged in St Albans, not far from where I grew up.

There was no peasant uprising when Stevenson walked this way, though agricultural labouring wages remained low. As the 1870s drew to a close, cheaper grain was being imported from Europe and North America, triggering a depression in farming that lasted until the 1940s and the war effort. In the Chilterns, land was abandoned, reverting to scrub. The depression came too late for the many miles of Chiltern hedgerows that were grubbed up when corn was profitable – much as they continued to be by twentieth-century agri-businesses. Between the 1870s, when Stevenson walked through the Chilterns, and 1945 there was very little hedgerow loss in Britain, with an estimated 500,000 miles of hedges in existence – most planted when the old open fields were enclosed. It's the decades since the war that have seen the greatest loss, with up to fifty percent now vanished. In 1997 legislation was passed to protect our hedgerows and the loss has slowed (though not halted), with farmers now incentivised to maintain hedges rather than cut them down.

Farming might have declined in the late nineteenth century, but with the extension of the Metropolitan Railway to the Chilterns in the 1880s, commuter towns and their surrounding villages flourished.

Lured by the lush brochure,
down byways beckoned,
To build at last the cottage of our dreams,
A city clerk turned countryman again,
And linked to the Metropolis by train.

John Betjeman, *Metro-Land*, 1973

My father was one such 'city clerk turned countryman again', though he'd already had a career travelling the world as an army officer. He'd started life as the grandson of a London drayman and only child of a shopkeeper in Exeter. He could so easily have stayed on in his hometown, and taken over the surgical appliances shop that my grandfather ran. But my father was clever, and he studied hard. He left Devon for Berkshire, and the Royal Military Academy Sandhurst, rising through the ranks of the army to become a major. After twenty years he renounced army life to work for a blue-chip American corporation. We relocated to Buckinghamshire, first renting a house in Chesham, then 'lured by the lush brochure' buying one in the nearby village of Ashley Green, two miles from where the Metropolitan Line terminates at Chesham.

The house my parents bought, and in which they still live today, is one of a row of five built between the end of the 1950s and the early 1960s. This was a time when England was nostalgic for a peaceful pre-war existence, turning against the soulless aesthetic of Modernist architecture that flourished between the wars. The soggy English climate never really suited the flat-roofed Modernist style, and nor did the extrovert nature of Modernism suit the English psyche, which values privacy and seclusion above all. Modernism just wasn't cosy enough, it seems.

It was this comforting pastoral dream that the builders of our family home tapped into when they developed the farmland along our lane. The estate agent's details from 1969, when my parents bought the house, describe it as:

> 'A most attractive DETACHED HOUSE of exceptional character, built only eight years ago by the well-known local firm of builders – Messrs. F. G. Whitman & Son, to their usual high standard of construction. The property has unusually attractive "cottage" style elevations, with second-hand stock bricks, the upper elevations being hung with old mature tiles under a patterned mature-tiled roof. The property backs onto open farmland, with delightful distant views across woodland.'

The picture this description conjures up is of a rural idyll, and it continues in much the same vein. 'The village shop and church are within a few minutes' walk, and there is an adequate bus service to Chesham and Berkhamsted Town Centres with their excellent shopping facilities' – and now the clincher that must have made up my parents' minds to buy the house – 'and train service to London (Baker Street 45 minutes, Euston 35 minutes)'. The asking price for living this rustic dream was £10,400. And so my father's life as a commuter, and ours as Metro-Land children, began.

For the next twenty years my mother dutifully drove my father to Berkhamsted station each weekday morning from where he would catch the train to Euston, and every evening she returned to collect him. My brother and I sometimes accompanied her on the evening run, and we always spotted him among the river of crumpled suits, straight-backed from his army training, his silhouette distinctive even in the gloom of winter evenings. Then, at weekends, his posture would soften, unfurling as he worked in the garden or washed the family car.

There was still Stevenson's 'bustle of autumn field-work' behind the hedgerows as I continued along Kings Lane that afternoon. Not the agricultural labourers that he found, but pylon workers, hard-hatted and in hi-vis jackets, clambering the iron pillars like mountaineers. Their shouts rang across the meadows, mingling with a jet engine overhead. The fields below were still as Stevenson described them – 'like a map'. Just like the 1620 map, in fact, that Alison Doggett had shown me, its collage of greens and browns a rumpled patchwork of muted autumn colours.

The English landscape, intricate as the finest lace, cannot be rushed. It is best absorbed at walking pace. All around, if you look hard enough, you notice traces of our forebears – in the copses, the hedges and the fields – reaching back through the centuries, each landmark telling its own story. For a moment I stood gazing over the valley. The din of men and planes faded and the familiar landscape of my youth was spread out before me like a tapestry, sewn over millennia and in places threadbare. A child of the Chilterns, I too was a thread in that tapestry, part of its warp and its weft.

A little further along the lane an old agricultural roller lay rusting in the corner of a field, entangled with grass and bracken. Did its owner just leave it there one day, meaning to come back and collect it? Or perhaps he grasped that the old way of life was disappearing and he'd no longer have need of it? On through an artery of high, sheltering hedges, tipped with russet and gold. Glimpses through gaps in the hedgerow of the deserted fields and meadows beyond, far from the 'fair fields full of folk' as witnessed in the medieval allegorical poem *The Vision of Piers Plowman*. These old beech hedges had been laid by hand, woven like the straw plaits made by the womenfolk of Potter Row. As the great landscape historian W G Hoskins said in his classic *The Making of the English Landscape*, hedges represent 'the physical evidence of decisions made long ago and fixed solidly on the ground'. Even though I could see no-one working in the fields, I sensed the presence of the generations before me who worked this land, planting, braiding and nurturing these dignified old hedgerows.

As usual, the Chilterns Conservation Board had the facts and figures. In a survey carried out in 2006–07, it estimated that the Chilterns AONB contains over 2,500 miles of old hedgerows. Historically, they served two main purposes: to delineate a political or territorial boundary (e.g. a parish boundary) and to control livestock. In the Chilterns, a high proportion started life as 'assart' hedges – lines of trees and shrubs left when areas of woodland were cleared for grazing or cultivation. Although 'ancient' hedges are officially defined as those which were in existence before the Enclosure Acts (1720–1840), the first documentary references for some Chiltern hedgerows are found in Anglo-Saxon charters. One such is Black Hedge, which formed the boundary of Monks

Risborough and was first mentioned in 903 during the reign of Edward the Elder, son of Alfred the Great, making it one of the oldest surviving hedgerows in England.

During the millennium since Britain's most ancient hedges were first planted they have grown to incorporate over six hundred plant species, home to around 1,500 species of insects, sixty-five species of birds and twenty species of mammals. In the Chilterns, these include song thrushes, linnets, tree sparrows, brown hares, dormice, stag beetles and bats. Thirty-eight of the animal species associated with Chiltern hedgerows are UK Biodiversity Action Plan priority species, says the Conservation Board. No wonder conservationists and campaigners against HS2 are so upset about their loss.

Living as I do now in the scarified Yorkshire Dales landscape of bare stone walls, the old hedgerows fringing Kings Lane certainly seemed ancient and opulent, reaching out to caress me as I walked between them. If I looked closely enough, in an old Chiltern hedgerow such as this I could expect to discover blackthorn, hazel and hawthorn – their blossom like strawberries and cream in spring. I might also unearth holly and honeysuckle, dog rose and dogwood, wild cherry and whitebeam. Interspersed with the hedge I'd find trees such as ash, hornbeam, beech and pedunculate (English) oak.

And I did indeed find English oak. I was passing through a whole avenue of them here in Kings Lane, standing guard like sentries, the wind aspirating through the leaf canopy. I counted my steps. These oaks stood around ten paces apart as if deliberately planted this way. In all likelihood, they were already growing here at the time the hedge was made. The landowners would have left them where they were, possibly as eventual sources of timber, while trees growing in inconvenient places would have been grubbed out.

> The great plain stretched away to the northward, variegated near at hand with the quaint pattern of the fields, but growing ever more and more indistinct, until it became a mere hurly-burly of trees and bright crescents of river, and snatches of slanting road, and finally melted into the ambiguous cloud-land over the horizon. The sky was an opal-grey, touched here and there with blue, and with certain faint russets that looked as if they were reflections of the colour of the autumnal woods below.

In Stevenson's time, the view he describes so lyrically was not blighted by busy bypasses, whining jet engines and buzzing pylons. I gazed across the Misbourne Valley at the 'quaint pattern of the fields', covering my ears to blot out the twenty-first-century din. Not only did I wish to see the landscape as Stevenson must have seen it, but I wanted to hear it as he must have heard it, too.

There was a public footpath leading into a recently harvested field, an old track that ran down the hillside to the A413 humming faintly below. I followed it for a while, and as I reached the pylons paused, acutely aware that I was standing in the middle of a railway line. In just a few years from now, trains would be screaming past me at just this spot every few minutes at deafening speed.

HS2 Ltd admits that noise from the trains at twenty-five metres away – about where I was standing – will be ninety-five decibels. Ninety-seven decibels is the sound of a newspaper press, or a Boeing 737 just before landing. This put the current intrusions of modern life – the roads, the pylons, the planes – into stark perspective. Robert Louis Stevenson, child of the Victorian era of progress and of civil engineers, may have endorsed this colossal infrastructure project. But Robert Louis Stevenson the nature lover and poet, who once walked across these same hills, would surely not.

There was an innocence about this stubbly field where I stood, cultivated over centuries by farmers such as Robert Brown. No premonition of what was to come, no sense of foreboding. Just serenity, as I looked down on the valley, its chequerboard of lanes and fields. This was absolutely Stevenson's 'quaint pattern of fields', which according to my 1880s map haven't changed since he was here. And which, according to Dame Mary Wolley's map, have altered little since 1620 – and probably much longer. Throughout the centuries, changes to this landscape have been incremental. The transformation about to arrive in these soft hills and yielding valleys will be sudden and dramatic, and the tranquil Chilterns of my childhood memories lost forever.

I returned to Kings Lane – but not for long, as Bowood Lane soon beckoned. This was another of Alison Doggett's 'delicious' little lanes, sinking down the hillside, fringed with bracken, dark and tunnel-like. Just like a cocoon, it enfolded me as I walked. According to HS2 Ltd's current plans, Bowood Lane will be sliced by a 100-metre cutting here, and a new bridge built over the railway line. I tried not to envisage this as I continued down the narrowing lane, noticing instead the remnants of summer flora in the hedgerows – vetch, and the blossoming rosebay willowherb in Alison's photo now turning an autumn auburn. The lane sank further into the earth and its ancient banks now rose above my head, to two or three times my height, almost blotting out the sun. Like the deep Etruscan roads of western Tuscany or the winding canyons of Petra, these are secret passageways linking ancient settlements, hidden from strangers' eyes.

But even these womb-like lanes could not muffle the roar of the A413 as I descended further into the valley, coiling between medieval field boundaries. The autumn sun was milky-soft now as I passed Wendover Dean Farm, its barn weather-boarded, its roof red-tiled and sagging, its façade wisteria-clad. The farm itself will be spared by HS2, though the concrete viaduct overhead will dominate this historic landscape, straddling the valley, and the noise from the trains will drown out the rumble of traffic from the A413.

Durham Farm, next door, will not be so fortunate. The plan is to demolish the entire farmstead, currently operating as an arable and cattle business, in order to construct the viaduct, rendering the farm unviable. To return to Kings Lane, and my way to Wendover, I needed to pass through Durham Farm on a public footpath that climbed steeply uphill. This was the last time I would climb this path, and a sadness enveloped me like the gathering dusk. I did not need to make this meandering detour off my route, but felt compelled to do so – a pilgrimage in homage and valediction to the mellow landscape of my youth. I didn't just want to see it with my eyes, I wanted to feel it beneath my feet.

> I could hear the ploughmen shouting to their horses, the uninterrupted carol of larks innumerable overhead, and, from a field where the shepherd was marshalling his flock, a sweet tumultuous tinkle of sheep-bells. All these noises came to me very thin and distinct in the clear air. There was a wonderful sentiment of distance and atmosphere about the day and the place.

The clocks had not yet gone back, and there was still light in the sky as I reached Kings Lane again, watched by a bemused flock of sheep. No shepherd marshalling this flock, although I passed a dilapidated shepherd's hut where he might once have lodged when his sheep were lambing. In use since the late Middle Ages, shepherds' huts reached their zenith in the late nineteenth century – just when Stevenson walked here – before declining as farming became increasingly mechanised. They've recently enjoyed a revival, commanding eye-watering prices as glamping pads, summerhouses or even writing huts for ex-prime ministers penning their memoirs.

There was an autumnal melancholy in the air, the sensation that not only the day but the year was ending. The sun, though still warm, was leaving the northern hemisphere on its trajectory south, and I was yet to hear Stevenson's 'uninterrupted carol of larks innumerable overhead'. I passed a whitewashed cottage where the owner had helpfully painted a sign showing the route of the public footpath. This led through the trimly mown garden down into the valley with its swathes of greens and swirls of greys, ribbons of woodland clasping the far slopes. My map informed me this path was the Chiltern Way, a long-distance circular footpath encompassing all four counties of the Chilterns from Bedfordshire in the east to Oxfordshire in the west, passing through Hertfordshire and Buckinghamshire *en route*. I was tempted to follow it downhill for one last foray into this serene vale before the bulldozers arrived, but the light was seeping from the sky and I was still some way from that night's destination. So I kept to Kings Lane, and soon the hedges closed in again to screen my final view of a valley so little altered for over four hundred years.

On past another pretty cottage, where the owner smiled at me as I went by, wishing me a good afternoon. I was tempted to ask her how she felt about losing her bucolic view over the Misbourne Valley, but it seemed too cruel a question on this soothing autumn afternoon. So I continued on to the hamlet of Kings Ash, another ash-themed place name. In the Chilterns, as elsewhere, this native broadleaf makes up around a third of woodland and hedgerow trees yet is now succumbing to ash dieback, a sickness that threatens to devastate the species in this country, just as Dutch elm disease did in the 1970s.

Caused by the fungus *Chalara fraxinea*, ash dieback in Britain was first detected in a nursery in East Anglia in early 2012. The trees had been imported from the Netherlands, globalisation breaching the natural barrier that the English Channel once served. Having brought about widespread damage to trees across Europe, it is likely that within the next few decades the disease will wreak similar destruction on the British ash population. Botanists estimate that we could lose around eighty million trees, and the plants and animals that depend on them for their survival. Like the vanished elm, ash trees figure prominently in English landscape poetry, especially verse about the Home Counties. As I walked along Kings Lane, John Betjeman's catchy lines kept pace with my footsteps:

Up the ash-tree climbs the ivy,
Up the ivy climbs the sun,
With a twenty-thousand pattering
Has a valley breeze begun,
Feathery ash, neglected elder,
Shift the shade and make it run –

John Betjeman, 'Upper Lambourne', 1940

At Kings Ash, Kings Lane swerved sharply left, becoming Chesham Lane – the last of those medieval thoroughfares twisting down to the valley bottom. Unlike Leather and Bowood lanes, Chesham Lane has not remained silently single-track, and no grass poked through its tarmac. Nor has it, like others I passed on my journey along Kings Lane, lapsed into a foot or bridle path, used only by farmers, riders and walkers. Chesham Lane, or Rocky Lane as it's locally known, is now a busy B-road. Instead of grass, white dotted lines now run along its middle as it carries traffic down the hillside to the even-busier A413. The old Kings Lane, or at least its course, continues straight on towards Wendover, and this is the route I now followed. Past an ash tree and into the woodland it went, road returning to track, asphalt to earth.

> The hills about Wendover and, as far as I could see, all the hills in Buckinghamshire, wear a sort of hood of beech plantation … But the autumn had scarce advanced beyond the outworks; it was still almost summer in the heart of the wood; and as soon as I had scrambled through the hedge, I found myself in a dim green forest atmosphere under eaves of virgin foliage. None of the trees were of any considerable age or stature; but they grew well together, I have said; and as the road turned and wound among them, they fell into pleasant groupings and broke the light up pleasantly.

We cannot know if Stevenson passed through this particular wood, wending his way to Wendover. But the town still wears a 'hood of beech plantation' on its hilly slopes before the Chilterns fall away into the Vale of Aylesbury. At this point, Kings Lane becomes Hogtrough Lane, an echo of the rural past – and of my own vanished past. In Ashley Green my home was on Hog Lane, although there are no hogs living among the executive houses now. But Hog Lane was where I spent my teenage summers, rambling and daydreaming between verges effervescent with cow parsley and frothy meadowsweet. The same rampant herb observed by the poet Edward Thomas as his express-train drew up in Adlestrop one late June afternoon in 1914, 'unwontedly'.

Thomas wrote these lines about his Cotswold rail journey three years after he, too, walked through the Chiltern Hills.

But the landscape he described, the 'willows, willow-herb, and grass/And meadowsweet, and haycocks dry', could as well have been written about the Chilterns. Despite the municipally mown verges and the smart barn conversions, you can still see many of the same wildflowers today in Chiltern commuter villages, still sense the old world veiled beneath the new.

Hogtrough Lane entered Barn Wood, so my Ordnance Survey map told me. The 1880s map, however, told me a different story, as although Barn Wood is marked it was far smaller then than it is today. This must be an example of agricultural land returning to woodland, as Alison Doggett described. Certainly, it would explain Stevenson's observation that 'none of the trees were of any considerable age or stature'. As with elm, ash, oak, hazel, holly and elder, beech is a relative latecomer to these islands. Like these other temperate broadleaved species, beech arrived after the last Ice Age – around eight to nine thousand years ago, when Britain was still connected to the continent by land.

For much of the following few thousand years, beech was not common, only later becoming widely spread due to deliberate planting. It was during the Iron Age that it spread across Britain, when the timber was used as fuel and to make charcoal, as in Coleman's Wood, and latterly for making furniture. Yet although beech appears to be the predominant species around here, as Stevenson found, it is not an easy tree to cultivate. It will only grow under the shelter of other trees and in well-drained soil.

Here, in Barn Wood, there are older trees growing alongside the beeches. This is a veteran path, hollowed and trodden deep by centuries of feet and hooves, bounded by age-old hedgerows, a tangle of oak, holly and beech. Contorted roots protruded from high banks. Beeches arched above my head, and last autumn's leaves crumbled under my feet. Doubtless hogs will once have feasted on the beechmast in Hogtrough Lane, fattening themselves for winter. The track was sinking steeply, now deep below tree-root level, and I soon became aware that the path I was walking on is truly historic – for here Hogtrough Lane is also the Ridgeway, an ancient trackway often described as Britain's oldest road.

Beginning (or ending) at Avebury in the north Wiltshire Downs the current Ridgeway National Trail ends (or begins) at Ivinghoe Beacon, a prominent Chiltern landmark topped by an Iron-Age hill fort:

Hoe: 'a sloping ridge or spur of land, promontory';
from Old English *hōh*

The original route that today's footpath incorporates is very much older, and very much longer. Possibly in use five thousand years ago, the old trackway (or series of trackways) followed high, chalky ground across the south of England, probably extending as far as East Anglia where it becomes the Icknield Way. It was walked and ridden by herdsmen and tradesmen, soldiers and travellers, and was still in use in the seventeenth century as a section of the road between London and Bath, before being superseded by the turnpike A4, and finally the M4 motorway.

Steeper and steeper the gradient as the chalk track rolled off the Chilterns into Wendover, pulling me down off the plateau. On the banks clumps of pink autumn cyclamen entwined with the ivy, the earth damp and musty, gorged with crushed leaves. Earth, flint and now chalk crunched beneath my boots.

As I neared Wendover, and left the wood behind, flocks of fat sheep munched on rich late-summer pasture. Then came St Mary's Church, banished like Great Missenden's to the edge of the town and dislocated from its community. A handsome flint building flanked by its trimmed yews, it nevertheless had a forlorn Monday air – no bustling women serving cream teas here. Then, just as I arrived alone and unnoticed, the church bell struck the hour as if to welcome me to Wendover. A patter of rain fell about my feet. Pulling the hood over my head, I quickened my step and hurried towards the centre of town.

The Farmer

From the Red Lion Hotel in Wendover I called my parents, who live only fifteen minutes away. Would they mind doing me a small favour by driving me back up the hill so I could go and talk to a farmer? I felt like a teenager again, asking to be collected from a friend's house, or rescued from an awkward adolescent party. Forty years had passed but they still didn't mind acting as my private taxi service, and turned up at the inn to drive me back to Hunts Green Farm so I could keep my appointment with Robert Brown.

It was barely light when I arrived. Robert was working in the farmyard, and summoned me over to his Mitsubishi pick-up. I climbed in, and we bumped and rattled through the yard and into the fields as Robert talked.

'That's where the train goes – in a straight line, virtually, with these pylon wires,' he said, pointing into the distance. 'And this cottage is where the night watchman is. They have a night watchman down here because the pylon cables are so expensive.'

'Who owns the cottage?' I asked.

'HS2 bought it. They paid about £1.2 million for it, and now they're renting it back to the people who owned it. It's an old cottage, and it was once a quarter of the size. It was called Three Bears Cottage, and it was a German prisoner-of-war camp. A German lady brought up nine children in there.'

Tucked away in its scrap of bosky woodland, Three Bears Cottage looked just like somewhere that Hansel and Gretel might have lived.

'Now, if you look over there now, down Leather Lane, you'll see two small trees, and in between there's a white post that sticks up – that's the top of the cutting. And it goes down to that plantation of trees.'

We looked out over the still-green fields at the white post in the distance.

'It goes from that dell, where that wooden thing is there that's the bottom side of the line, and the top side is where that marker is, up Leather Lane. So if we go down a little bit more, we're going to be right in the middle of it.'

We bumped and rattled some more, over the fields, until the pick-up jolted to a halt.

'This is now about the middle of the line. And it cuts right through Grim's Ditch, there.'

Around 350 metres of the ancient earthwork is etched onto Robert Brown's land, and around 150 metres of this will soon be flattened by HS2. But, as Buckinghamshire Archaeological Society claims, not only will this 150-metre section be destroyed but a whole tract of buried history will become a spoil heap. As the society concludes, 'the heavy earthmoving equipment will just as surely destroy what is left'.

We pulled up alongside a swathe of woodland.

'I can show you the ditch because this pylon lot have had to cut it out because of doing the wires,' said Robert. 'You can see it very easily now.'

Scrambling out of the pick-up we walked towards the woodland, aiming for a bare patch recently stripped of trees by the pylon workers. A large cable left by the workers snaked across our path, like a python ready to strike. Robert Brown was not perturbed.

'This is Grim's Ditch here. Let's just walk over this wire…'

'Careful! It might be live!'

'It shouldn't be.'

We stepped over the cable, and I spotted a distinctive dip and shallow bank amongst the trees. Robert pointed at the earthwork. 'It goes right up through the wood, across that field. The pylon people got strict rules from English Heritage that they weren't allowed to touch anything within so-many metres of Grim's Ditch.'

'But that's where they're putting the railway!'

'The train's going right through the middle. So how do you make sense of that? Anyone around here in the last several years who's wanted to put an extension on their house or build a conservatory, Chiltern District Council is dead against it – "it's an Area of Outstanding Natural Beauty" – and they're going to allow a train to come right through the middle of it all.'

I took a photo with my phone. 'It's such a pity they've cut all these trees down, but on the other hand it's fantastic that you can actually see Grim's Ditch.'

'Yes, and it's going to be bulldozed. Now, we'll just shoot across here because you will see the landscape that HS2's going to ruin.'

'You must feel horrible about it.' I felt pretty horrible about it, too.

Robert wanted to show me where the spoil from the tunnel will be dumped. According to the HS2 Amersham Action Group, the heap will be on prime arable land, with an estimated forty-eight percent used by HS2 during the construction period and a permanent total loss of around fourteen percent. An adjacent bird reserve will be severely impacted, and any dumping between March and July will have an effect on young birds that take refuge in the pasture. Nearly two million tonnes of tunnel spoil will be deposited at Hunts Green Farm. Unless HS2 Ltd come up with a better plan, its eventual removal will involve an estimated 63,000 lorry movements, and will take four years. It will take another five years to restore the land. It was hard to take in these figures.

We drove into a meadow, still sprinkled with clover and other summery wildflowers. It's what the naturalists call a 'dense, multi-species sward'.

'These are all meadows that haven't been touched for over a hundred years,' said Robert Brown. 'You can make lovely hay out of that. We haven't fertilised it, we do it all with sheep. We haven't finished haymaking yet this year because the weather has been so awful.'

'Maybe we'll get an Indian summer,' I replied. 'We deserve one.'

Robert drove me in a sweep around the meadow. 'We cut hay in the middle, but all round the outside we do haylage or silage for the cattle, because you can't make hay under trees.' The meadow, plus the arable fields he showed me earlier, are the core of his business. But as we continued our tour of his land, it became clear that the farm meant more to him than just commerce. We looked towards the woods fringing his meadow.

'These are all badgers' holes. This is a big area for badgers, and that wood is full of them – we call it Brick Wood.' I wondered whether the original name was in fact Brock Wood, 'brock' being the old country name for a badger. Either way, it was nice to meet a farmer who really cared for the land – and I told him so.

'To be honest with you, I try to do everything as naturally as I can. Now when the haymaking's finished, this field will have sheep on it. Sheep do it the world of good because they bring the grass right down so any old grass that's a bit oldie-woldie, they eat it, and then you get fresh new grass to make lovely hay. Also, they poo all over it, so it's got fertiliser too.'

'Historic permanent pasture' is the expert's term for such a meadow. Since World War II, ninety-seven percent of Britain's original hay meadows have been lost. Before too long, Robert Brown's will add to the tally. I took one last look at it before he swung the pick-up round, back towards the farm.

'The train line cuts through those grass fields we've just come up. And it goes straight on, in a line with those pylons, to Wendover.'

'I can't believe this beautiful countryside is going to be destroyed...'

'Yeah. And it's a good job we've come round this way because the buggers have left the gate open tonight. I've got keys so if you don't mind, I'm going to lock it up, and then we're back to the farm.'

After he locked the gate the pylon workers had left open we drove back to the farmyard, where my parents were waiting in the car. But before I left, Robert had a few final thoughts on HS2 to share with me.

'Two of my big arable fields that I grow bread-making wheat on, which is all food for the public, will go. But we've got a bigger population and we're losing farmland. You can keep building, but you'll never get the farmland back. So in a few years to come there will probably be food rationing.' Losing his two best fields will probably render Robert Brown's entire farm unviable. This agricultural perspective is one you don't often hear when housing developments or infrastructure projects such as HS2 are debated. It takes a die-hard farmer to see the wider picture.

'It only wants that volcanic dust, like several years ago in Iceland if you remember, and all the aircraft were grounded for two days,' continued Robert Brown. 'Fruit and vegetables didn't get here. People panic buy and the supermarkets were empty. Queuing for your food is around the corner. You can't keep taking land out of production that feeds a population.'

I opened the pick-up's door to say goodbye, aware of my parents waiting nearby and the skies darkening. But Robert was still in full flow, his exasperation at the folly of HS2 showing little sign of abating.

'I'm all for progress, but the thing is we'll have no benefit from the train here. Anyway, there's not the call for people to get anywhere quicker like ten years ago because now they've all got their computers on their laps.'

I nodded in agreement. 'What we really need is faster broadband. Where I live in North Yorkshire, we only have two megabytes.'

'Yeah. So they've got their computers on their laps, they've got phones that do everything, there's not the need for anybody to get there faster. The people going into London if they want to work they can work the minute they get on the train.' I cast my mind back to Keith Hoffmeister, who said exactly the same thing to me just a few days before. Robert Brown's valedictory words were almost out of earshot as I shut the door.

'And to be running as regularly as they are – there's going to be no call for it, so it's a white elephant. That's what it is, a white elephant.'

DAY THREE

Wendover to Tring

Wendover, in itself, is a straggling, purposeless sort of place. Everybody seems to have had his own opinion as to how the street should go; or rather, every now and then a man seems to have arisen with a new idea on the subject, and led away a little sect of neighbours to join in his heresy.

Wendover: 'white waters' (chalk stream); from Brittonic *Wændofran* (c. 970)

Tumbling down its hillside, Wendover isn't a 'straggling, purposeless sort of place' anymore. Today, it's a wealthy commuter town from which Chiltern Railways shuttles its besuited cargo into and out of London Marylebone each day. Although Wendover is bypassed to the west by the A413 that links Great Missenden and Aylesbury, traffic continues to rumble down the High Street, which doubles as the B4009 between Newbury in Berkshire and Tring in Hertfordshire.

Squinting through their windscreens at the road ahead, the drivers of these cars and lorries will barely notice the old buildings lining the High Street: the timber-framed and brick houses, the sagging tiled roofs, the bulging façades, the towering chimney stacks of this historic market town.

One such timber-framed façade conceals the Red Lion Hotel, where I ended my previous day's walk. Almost a century and a half later, it's still recognisable as the 'pleasant old house, with bay-windows, and three peaked gables, and many swallows' nests plastered about the eaves' of Stevenson's description. The inn has been rather extended since then, and the swallows' nests have long since been cleared away by tidy-minded townsfolk.

Also not so apparent today are the 'white waters', the chalk stream (or 'bourne' in this neck of the beech woods) after which Wendover was named by pre-Anglo-Saxon Britons, and which determined this settlement's location on the lip of the Chiltern escarpment. The original stream was channelled in 1799 to become the Wendover Arm, which supplied water for the Grand Union Canal, but you can still find its original source near the Church of St Mary. Like so many Christian sites of worship the church was built on pagan foundations, the new religion supplanting the old. For water meant life, and springs were holy places. Chalk streams mean life today too, for *Ranunculus aquatilis*, or freshwater crowfoot (a relative of the buttercup) that supports a range of invertebrates and provides cover for fish. They also create habitat for water voles – a species in drastic decline across the whole country. With eighty-five percent of the world's two hundred chalk streams found in England, these clear Chiltern bournes are indeed exceptional places.

It was to St Mary's Church on the edge of Wendover that I headed back that morning, retracing my steps to where I'd ended my walk the previous evening and to where the last leg of my journey across the Chiltern Hills began. A pall of cloud hung over the valley, shrouding the woods that clambered up the hillside beyond, the Forestry Commission conifers lending the town a misty, Alpine air.

HS2 will pass very close to Wendover as it will to Great Missenden. It will cross the A413, running parallel to the town and shaving the Wendover Memorial Woodland, planted in 2010 by a local hospice as a place for reflection and remembrance. The plan in Wendover is for a 'green tunnel'. This sounds innocent enough, but green tunnels are 'cut-and-covered', which means that the land will be removed for the cutting and then backfilled, effectively destroying everything in its path and ultimately more destructive than a mined tunnel. This not-so-green tunnel will possibly also cause structural damage to nearby Bacombe Hill, a Site of Special Scientific Interest renowned for butterflies, such as the chalkhill blue, and orchids like the fragrant orchid (*Gymnadenia conopsea*), both characteristic of this rare, open chalky grassland. But it is the Bronze Age 'bell barrow' tumulus (burial mound), a Scheduled Ancient Monument on top of Bacombe Hill, that most concerns conservationists and archaeologists, who fear that construction of HS2 will cause the structure to become unstable.

Eventually the line will be separated from the town by the so-called Wendover Wall, a military-style barrier almost double the height of the former Berlin Wall which is supposed to screen off the worst of the noise from Wendover's inhabitants. HS2 Ltd claims that noise from the trains, even where three-metre high barriers are in place, will be seventy-six decibels, although campaigners against HS2 believe these estimates fall short of reality. Seventy-six decibels is the sound of an average vacuum cleaner, or a car passing at sixty-five miles per hour.

But I'd seen enough the previous day of the havoc HS2 will wreak in my Chiltern homeland. That morning I wanted to stride out across the hills and the meadows one last time, as summer faded and autumn took hold. Above all, I really wanted to hear a skylark. The air might not have been 'alive with them from High Wycombe to Tring' as it was for Stevenson but surely I should hear at least one before the end of my walk. And I was at least walking this last leg. As Stevenson cheerfully admits in 'In the Beechwoods':

> The morning cleared a little, and the sky was once more the old stone-coloured vault over the sallow meadows and the russet woods, as I set forth on a dog-cart from Wendover to Tring.

Stevenson was, in Victorian parlance, a sickly youth. Like so many of his contemporaries, he was thought to have been suffering from tuberculosis ('consumption'), although medical experts today dispute that he had this disease, or at least that he died from it. Besides, to play the role of a romantically ailing poet was the height of late nineteenth-century fashion, which may also have played a role in Stevenson's decision not to walk the final day of his Chiltern jaunt.

No dog-cart to hand, and preferring to walk anyway, I struck off down a minor road which my OS map told me was Hale Lane. The map also informed me I was now walking on the Icknield Way. Along with the Ridgeway, this is one of the oldest trackways in Britain.

Icknield: Icenhylte (c. 903); Brittonic, from the Iceni tribe of East Anglia

Tracing the chalk spine of England, from East Anglia to Dorset, the Icknield Way was first mentioned in Anglo-Saxon charters. In the eleventh century, Edward the Confessor gave its travellers royal protection, and it finally became an official long-distance leisure path in 1992. The path's official starting point is Ivinghoe Beacon and it ends in Suffolk – at 112 miles somewhat shorter than its original, Iron Age incarnation when it was a significant road for livestock droving and flint trading.

You see these flints everywhere in the Chilterns still, half-buried in the clay topsoil and a hallmark of my childhood rambles. Sometimes, these nodules of stone would be whole, wrapped in a skin of chalk like a misshapen potato. But mostly they'd be broken open, revealing their glittery quartz innards which would glint through the earth like gems.

Flint is the traditional building material of the Chilterns, the 'knapped' surfaces often used to impressive decorative effect. Originating in chalky rock, flints are formed of silica and have been used since early Palaeolithic times to fashion tools and weapons such as axe-heads, arrow-heads and scrapers. Indispensable utensils, then, to the earliest inhabitants of these islands.

Knap: 'to knock, rap or strike sharply'; from Middle English *knappen*

Not many flint traders or livestock drovers navigate the Icknield Way's chalky course nowadays. Just walkers, riders and the occasional poet, drawn by the romance of this ancient route. One such poet was Edward Thomas who, in June 1911, just a few years before the Great War which was to claim his life, set out on a ten-day walk across the chalk downs of England. As when Stevenson walked here nearly forty years previously, the pre-war meadows were still crammed with wildflowers and the sky heavy with the chorus of birds, such as the skylark. On the day he passed through Tring and Wendover, Thomas describes how:

> the air was sweet now with roses, now with yellow bedstraw. Larks sang, and a yellowhammer that forgot the end of its song, and once a blackbird.

In the book he wrote about his walk, *The Icknield Way*, Thomas describes how, as it skirts the edge of the Chiltern escarpment, the route divides to become two parallel tracks: the Upper and Lower Icknield Way. Historically, the lower track was more direct, and suitable for summer traffic. In winter, travellers probably preferred the upper route, which ran further up the chalky escarpment and would have been drier.

It is the Upper Icknield Way that leads out of Wendover towards Tring. Unfortunately, the Upper Icknield Way is also the busy B4009, its prehistoric track long since buried under layers of tarmac. This was the route that Edward Thomas apparently took, but for the sake of safety and sanity I was following today's

Icknield Way trail. It wasn't easy to find among the suburbs of Wendover, so I asked a dog-walker the way. She couldn't tell me as she'd never walked to Tring – only five miles away as the kite flies. In Stevenson's time, anyone you met in the countryside would have known every path intimately. They would have understood how each village, hamlet and farm were connected. Now, most people walk their dogs along these paths, then get into their cars to drive to the nearest town. Once, an invisible thread of human kinship fastened the communities of Wendover and Tring. Now the car, travelling along its narrow asphalt corridor, has unravelled it.

Retracing my steps I passed rows of bungalows, gardens planted with rows of dazzling geraniums. Their lawns were clipped, their flowerbeds were neat and the damp valley clay was sown with well-spaced annuals. From high leylandii came the fat, lazy, coo of wood pigeons. A comfortable, complacent, Home Counties sound – so different from the thin, trilling call of the curlew, the wading bird which soars above the moorland surrounding my Yorkshire home. Coming from these gentle slopes and valleys of the Chilterns I had no idea what a curlew was when we first arrived in the Yorkshire Dales, this mottle-brown bird with spindly legs and long curved beak. But soon I learned to love its ecstatic, trilling call and now mark the date of its arrival each year in the calendar. For along with the snowdrops, the crocuses and the daffodils, the curlew is the undeniable herald of spring in the moorlands of North Yorkshire. Yet like the skylark, its numbers are declining rapidly and it could soon disappear altogether from the British countryside.

After various false starts, I eventually found Hale Lane and the open road once again. Either side of Hale Lane fields of autumn stubble billowed and swelled, an artist's palette of pale ochres and raw siennas, of burnt umbers and brown madders. Ahead, as the road rose softly up the slope of the escarpment, pastureland was crowned with bronzing beech hangars. Native cranesbill geraniums, violet blue, still sprinkled the late summer verges, their subtle hue a gentle rebuke to their brash Mediterranean cousins in Wendover's suburbs. Rosebay willowherb, leaves tinged with autumn scarlet, pink clover, blue scabious and gold dandelions daubed the roadside, whilst the stubble prairies beyond were barren and flowerless. It's not in the modern fields that you see vestiges of old England now – it's in the verges, the margins, the borders.

> The fields were busy with people ploughing and sowing; every here and there a jug of ale stood in the angle of the hedge, and I could see many a team wait smoking in the furrow as ploughman or sower stepped aside for a moment to take a draught. Over all the brown ploughlands, and under all the leafless hedgerows, there was a stout piece of labour abroad, and, as it were, a spirit of picnic.

Stevenson, a chain smoker throughout his life, had noticed the plough-teams smoking in the furrows. He would not then have known the damage his own roll-up cigarettes were doing to his already weak lungs, although it was a brain haemorrhage that eventually killed him just twenty years after his Chiltern journey.

This morning, almost 150 years after that journey, the fields along Hale Lane were not so busy with 'people ploughing and sowing'. A solitary tractor passed as I walked towards the brow of the hill. Somewhere, from behind a hedgerow not yet leafless, drifted the whirr and clank of farm machinery. Someone was still working the fields, perhaps drilling them for winter wheat – one person taking the place of the dozens that Stevenson saw working the land.

When it ripens in the summer not a weed will be seen amongst these rippling ears of winter wheat. Not a poppy. Not even a cornflower – those delicate blue blooms of the old agrarian landscape, named after the cornfields in which they grew, sapphires studding a crown of gold. Poppies and cornflowers reduce the purity, and therefore the value, of the wheat. This exhausted field will be sprayed with herbicide, and although the wheat should thrive, not much else will.

The melancholy autumn mist that had hung over Wendover had now dissolved, and I was in the sunny Chiltern uplands once again. Cloud shadows rolled across the jigsaw of fields and woods, like surf over sand, in waves of light and shade. There was a wistfulness to the late summer landscape, as if resigned to the autumn about to come. The wood at the top of the hill summoned me upward, towards The Hale.

Hale: 'corner, angle or nook of land'; from Old English *halh*, or *healh*

This hamlet was indeed in a corner of land, the lane kinking around it as it continued its progress up the hill. I paused to catch my breath and to admire a Georgian-fronted house in its walled garden before diving off left towards deep, dank beech woods. Here the footpath divided, and as inviting as it was for this daughter of the Chilterns, I decided not to follow the umbrous woodland way but instead continued uphill through an open meadow, scooped from the hillside and bathed in benign late summer sun. The turf was still springy underfoot, clover and buttercups still surged from the earth.

As with Robert Brown's hay meadow, this one had apparently never seen any ploughing, strimming or weed-killing. Almost all English hay meadows may have disappeared in the generation since I left the Chilterns, but here a fragment still remained: downy, soft, giving and forgiving. Pockets of unblemished landscape still exist even in this corner of crowded southeast England if you know where to look. And standing there I could quite see why my parents were content here in the Chilterns, this quasi-rural idyll, happy with their gentle walks through gentle woodland. I've become used to wilder landscapes now, used to being surrounded by sheep and curlews, by heather and gorse, but I envy them their Chiltern contentment, and their sense of belonging.

Autumn seemed very far away in that velvet pasture, enfolded by its woods. Damp grass pulled at my boots like wet sand, dew soaked through to my socks. I turned to look back over the hazed valley at the farmhouse below, and Wendover beyond. It was another of those rare moments when the modern world receded, the rumble of traffic faded and only birdsong filled the skies. Surely, if I was to hear a skylark before my walk ended, now was when I was going to hear it. Just one lark amidst the sonata above, and I'd be happy.

No skylark. I turned again, and continued towards the wood passing hedgerows heavy with rowan berries, chiffchaffs darting amongst the branches, and emerged via a cobweb of paths at a scattering of houses. Disorientated, I asked a brawny young man landscaping one of the gardens where I might be. And where might I find Grim's Ditch, the Iron Age earthwork I last saw in a corner of Robert Brown's land? You're in Lanes End, he replied, but he was Polish and didn't know about the ditch so he went to fetch the householder who pointed me in the right direction.

At Coppice Farm, a path led onto the course of Grim's Ditch which runs straight on for the next few miles, though there was no sense of it under this quiet lane. The sun warmed my shoulders despite the cool autumnal air and the rare, pale mauve Chiltern gentian (*Gentianella germanica*), Buckinghamshire's county flower, was still in bloom – summer's farewell. Hedgerows drooped with sloes, glistening darkest purple after the previous night's rain shower and begging to be plucked. A long-legged horse elegant as a ballerina looked up from an adjacent field as I passed, clouds of steam puffing from her nostrils. A more Arcadian Chiltern scene you couldn't imagine.

Reaching a crossroad, I continued along the line of the earthwork as marked on my OS map and entered a narrow strip of nameless woodland. It was exactly the same length and shape as on the 1880s map. Here, I found myself walking along the edge of an embankment, a definite trough to my right. This at last was Grim's Ditch as I remembered it from childhood, its name sounding faintly sinister to my impressionable ears. Grim's Ditch, or Grim's Dyke, is a series of linear earthworks that stretches over eleven miles of Buckinghamshire and Hertfordshire and was probably built as a boundary in the Bronze and Iron Ages. As Historic England states in its listing, 'The Buckinghamshire and Hertfordshire Grim's Ditch is thought to have served as a territorial boundary, separating, and perhaps enclosing, organised groups of land and settlement.' First mention of it was made in the late twelfth century, when it was referred to as Grimesdic. Grim, or Grymes, is the Anglo-Saxon name for a mysterious, ancient feature in the landscape, its origin apparently the Norse word *grimr*, or devil, or 'hooded one'. So Grim's Ditch means Devil's Ditch – no wonder it so perturbed me as a child.

Walking along Grim's Ditch today you sense a Chiltern landscape crosshatched with boundaries, from the Iron Age to the digital age. Tribal boundaries, county boundaries, parish boundaries score these supple hills, many superimposed one upon the other. We humans are obsessed with borders, with defining our territory, with keeping people out, whether waves of Celtic tribesmen three thousand years ago or waves of bricklayers from Eastern Europe today. Whether it's boundaries in Belfast or Berlin, Israel or Mexico, walking along a boundary, even one as ancient and inconsequential as Grim's Ditch, is defying mankind's attempts to create divisions. It's deciding to belong to neither one side nor the other, choosing to be, in the immortal words of Theresa May, 'a citizen of nowhere'.

This ancient ditch has now been shallowed by vegetation and by time, but as I scrambled down to its bottom I was diving three thousand years into the past. Here, close to the hamlet of Hastoe, the embanked ditch is around three and a half metres wide and two metres deep. It's impressive still, though would have been even more so three millennia ago when it was first dug. I clambered out again to continue along this prehistoric boundary, glimpsing through the trees the prairie fields of twenty-first century agriculture where no skylarks sang. But in this scrap of old woodland I was still submerged in the past, walking along a corridor of ancient history where nature still thrived.

My secretive woodland walk ended suddenly, and a sign ahead announced Dacorum Borough Council. After nearly three days I was leaving beechy Bucks and entering Hertfordshire.

Dacorum: 'Hundred of the Danes'; from Latin *Daci*, hundredo Dacorum (1196)

Dacorum is one of the 'Chiltern Hundreds'. Traditionally it refers to an administrative region that could raise one hundred men to fight on behalf of the Crown – but the word means something very different to me. The Dacorum Borough Council sign took me back forty years, and to the daily crossing of this boundary between Buckinghamshire, where I lived, and Hertfordshire, where I went to secondary school.

Crossing the Dacorum border to my new school in Berkhamsted was like entering a foreign land. Most of Ashley Green's kids – my fellow schoolmates – went on to Cestreham County Secondary School in nearby Chesham, which was in Buckinghamshire.

When I went in the opposite direction, to the more affluent Berkhamsted, our lives never converged again. I made new friends amongst my new classmates. The village kids, my former school chums from Snowhill Cottages with whom I used to gossip in the bus stop, now thought us 'posh' and so I became a foreigner in my own village.

Ashley Green's only purpose-built council estate, Snowhill Cottages, was thrown up in 1948 when the country needed to replace the near half-million houses lost during World War II. Many of these new council estates were raised on greenfield sites on the edges of Chiltern towns and villages. A safe thirty miles from London's grime and crime, these modest houses prospered as peaceful Home Counties retreats in the middle decades of the twentieth century, rubbing along with their grander detached neighbours. But today the Green Belt protecting this pastoral dream is steadily being eroded, and London's tentacles are almost within grasping distance.

Pleasant, semi-detached houses surrounded by proud little gardens, Snowhill Cottages were named in homage to their once-rural setting opposite Snowhill Farm. Some of the families that originally lived in them were doubtless employed across the road when it was still a working farm. Today, like so much social housing throughout England, they are no longer affordable homes for agricultural workers and labourers, having been sold off as private homes from the 1980s under Right to Buy. Now they fetch dizzying prices on the open market. And so continues the transformation of Ashley Green – like so many of its Chiltern neighbours – from a chiefly rural community after World War II to a largely commuter village in the early twenty-first century.

Below the Dacorum Borough Council notice, another sign advised me I was back on the Chiltern Way and pointed into a vast plain of cheerless rapeseed stubble. And it was here, not in the meadows filled with clover but in this desolate tract of farmland, that I heard for the very first time on my walk – a skylark. I stopped in my tracks. Could this be the bird I'd been listening for during the past three days? Scrambling for my phone, I played an audio clip from the RSPB's website. Yes, this was undoubtedly the song I was hearing around me so near my journey's end. Not quite Stevenson's 'wonderful carolling of larks' perhaps, but certainly a respectable chorus of them. And I could see them too, a flock of skylarks swooping amongst the stubble. Reading the RSPB's webpage furnished me with the bare facts:

> The skylark is a small brown bird, somewhat larger than a sparrow but smaller than a starling. It is streaky brown with a small crest, which can be raised when the bird is excited or alarmed, and a white-sided tail. The wings also have a white rear edge, visible in flight. It is renowned for its display flight, vertically up in the air. Its recent and dramatic population declines make it a Red List species.

Of course, I should have expected to see them in this humdrum agrarian environment rather than in the halcyon meadows of my imagination. The skylark is, after all, a farmland bird which nests in arable fields – particularly in open spaces so they can look out for predators. Skylarks would not have been nesting now, in late summer. Mostly likely, the birds were feeding on seeds and insects to fatten up for winter. But with greater efficiency in farming there's little seed spillage so skylarks – along with their fellow farmland birds – are finding their food supply running low. Lower still, with crops routinely doused in the herbicide glyphosate for a greater consistency of yield. This may be more cost-effective for the farmers, though it's at the expense of weed-loving insects, and the birds – including skylarks – who feed off them.

This, coupled with the fact that today's farmers tend to plough right to the margins of fields, is a double whammy for farmland birds. Since the 1970s bird numbers have declined hugely, with an estimated forty-four million pairs of breeding birds lost in the past forty years (that's around one million birds per annum). But the declines are most significant in farmland birds, pushed as they are to the very edges. When I was young, the birds seemed abundant and life – my life – equally abundant. Back then, I did not know what a skylark was. I did not feel the need to name the birds, identify the butterflies, classify the flowers. I thought that they, like me, would go on forever. As permanent as the elms. Now, as they disappear from the world, the urge to embed them in the mind, in the memory, is overwhelming. One day they, like the elms, may be gone, and only the memory of them will remain.

In fact, it's a triple whammy for the skylark, as perhaps the greatest harm to their existence is the current trend for winter wheat. Even *Farmer's Weekly* admits in an article published in 2000 that 'the switch from spring-sown to autumn-sown cereals over the past 30 years has been disastrous for the skylark'.

But, as the article continues, 'the National Farmers Union said that the move to autumn-sown cereals was brought about by the need for British agriculture to be competitive' and that 'farmers would be prepared to return to spring-sown cereals if they could be assured that [consumers] were prepared to pay more.' Meanwhile, as we wait for consumers to respond to this challenge, conservationists and lobbying groups such as the RSPB are persuading farmers to leave gaps in their arable fields for 'skylark plots': undrilled patches to encourage nesting and help alleviate what seems to be the inevitable avian apocalypse.

Skylark patches, autumn drilling, seed spillage. It's all too easy to become bogged down in these technical terms, and in doing so lose the romance of the skylarks while they're still around to share our countryside, and our imagination. For me, that day felt like a kind of redemption, a validation of my admittedly dwindling faith that I would hear at least one skylark on my Chiltern journey. And it was Shelley's ode to *Alauda arvensis* that came to mind as I left them to their carolling:

Teach me half the gladness
That thy brain must know,
Such harmonious madness
From my lips would flow
The world should listen then, as I am listening now.
Percy Bysshe Shelley, 'To a Skylark', 1820

Buoyant, and with a new spring in my step, I entered the last strip of woodland running alongside the edge of Grim's Ditch. So nearly did I take the alluring lower path at The Hale, and walk through the beech woods on the Ridgeway. So nearly did I miss hearing skylarks in the desiccated, stubbly prairies of the Chiltern plateau.

Grim's Ditch continues into the Wick Wood ahead, but it's here that I had to leave my natural habitat and turn a reluctant left, towards Tring and the final destination of my walk.

Wick: 'dwelling, farm or settlement'; from Latin *vicus*, Old English *wīc*, 'farm'

Tring was familiar territory, the next town along from Berkhamsted and the closest I'd be on my walk to Ashley Green. Not that there's much in it – Tring is a mile or so closer to my village than Great Missenden, a couple of miles nearer than Wendover. It was as if I'd spent the past three days treading in a wary semicircle around my past.

Marlin Hill, which winds down the hill to Tring, was living in the past too, clinging onto the last vestiges of summer. The hedgerows were fringed with vetch and rosebay willowherb, still in flower. Just before the final descent into Tring, a sign pointed right, to the Ridgeway footpath. A man ahead of me on the lane, a fellow walker with a rucksack on his back, turned onto this path. For a moment I hesitated, envying him, longing to follow him along the Chiltern escarpment rather than walk down the road to Tring, and my journey's finale.

And I did follow him, just for a while, before my path splintered off the Ridgeway and took me down through Tring Park towards the town. The last opportunity to walk through serene beech woods before entering the busy modern borough. Dropping steeply down the Chiltern ridge through landscaped parkland I saw Ivinghoe Beacon ahead, the end of the Icknield Way and Ridgeway long-distance paths.

Among the avenues of beech trees, cattle chewed grass to the accompaniment of noise from the A41 Tring bypass. This was the same road that I could hear from my old bedroom in my parents' house, the same road that was extended in the 1990s to detour around Berkhamsted, skimming the very edge of the Hockeridge Woods. Bypasses, housing estates, high-speed train lines: little by little, the Chiltern landscape is being carved up, its people and wildlife corralled into smaller and smaller spaces. And except for a few minutes now and again, almost my entire walk - unlike Stevenson's - had been to the aural backdrop of traffic or planes, like white noise.

Crossing the dual carriageway into Tring I walked down Park Road, a street lined with elegant Georgian villas and less elegant Victorian ones, and crossed Akeman Street, a Roman road linking the Roman cities of Bath and St Albans, and which marked, all too soon, the end of my Chiltern walk.

Tring: 'slope where trees grow'; from Old English *trēow* + *hangra*, Trehangr (1199)

Stevenson's journey had ended rather perfunctorily too, as if, unlike me, he couldn't wait to finish and get back to London – back to his mistress, and on to greater things.

> Tring was reached, and then Tring railway-station; for the two are not very near, the good people of Tring having held the railway, of old days, in extreme apprehension, lest some day it should break loose in the town and work mischief. I had a last walk, among russet beeches as usual, and the air filled, as usual, with the carolling of larks; I heard shots fired in the distance, and saw, as a new sign of the fulfilled autumn, two horsemen exercising a pack of fox-hounds. And then the train came and carried me back to London.

This was the end of my last day walking the Chilterns in the footsteps of Robert Louis Stevenson. But even if I'd not followed his exact route, I had still been pacing in the footsteps of all those who walked these paths when my old 1880s maps were made, and when Stevenson was walking here too.

So much has changed since then. Many of the topographical features appearing on the maps have been lost, such as the orchards around Hazlemere and Holmer Green, living on in house names only. Field boundaries have disappeared under the plough, and quiet lanes once dotted with farms are now busy roads fringed with housing. Other, once bustling, thoroughfares have reverted to footpaths used only by walkers and horse riders. And then there are the railways. Stevenson had noted that the 'good people of Tring' once held the London and Birmingham Railway 'in extreme apprehension'. How much more apprehensive must they be now, as a massive new rail project endangers their cherished Chiltern landscape?

But stepping beyond the roads and the railways, and walking deep into this landscape, you discover that much of the old England endures here. In the woods, groves and copses, many of which have retained their nineteenth-century size, shape and names. In the Misbourne Valley, the epicentre of my own Chiltern journey, where most of the old field boundaries remain – at least until HS2 slices through its ancient hedges and meadows. And in the sense of community that, while not underpinned by agriculture as in the old days, is cemented in a common cause brought on by the impending threat of HS2.

I'd been walking alone across the hills and had not found Stevenson's 'great coming and going of school-children upon by-paths,' or 'stout country-folk a-ploughing'. Yet never did I feel lonely. There was a real sense of companionship with the many thousands who had walked here before me: mostly farmers, but also merchants, drovers and labourers. And although I may not have been farming as my ancestors had, I was walking as they did, and by walking I had closed the gap between the generations. Whether my forebears came from the gentle hills and valleys of the Chilterns where I grew up, or the fells and dales of Yorkshire where I now live, they shared the same deep attachment to the land.

The Chilterns is not my home any more, but it's still my parents' home. When my father retired from his City job after twenty years commuting into London they decided to stay on in Ashley Green. Freed from the burden of office life, my father learned new languages, sat on tribunals, took up golf. My mother continued with her work at the Citizens Advice Bureau, which she'd begun some years before. Both threw themselves enthusiastically into parish life. My father joined the team who replaced the village's wobbly old stiles with robust new steel gates, very much like the one dedicated to Heather K Herrington at the entrance to Stockings Wood. He also helped clear the village footpaths of undergrowth – work which earned high commendation from the Chilterns Conservation Board in 2009. Like Britain in Bloom, communal efforts such as this knit together the social fabric of the Middle England where I grew up.

During these past three days across the Chilterns I'd reconnected with my past, and with the countryside of my youth – one that will never be the same once HS2 makes its mark here. Treading these paths after almost forty years, it seemed like forever since I left. But it also seemed like no time at all. And wherever I walk in the world, I will remember this Chiltern homecoming and sense again the same enduring bond with the chalky hills beneath my feet.

As for Robert Louis Stevenson, he left the Chilterns, and as far as I know never returned. Instead, he travelled in Europe and in 1878 published *An Inland Voyage*, about a canoe trip in France and Belgium. From Europe he journeyed to America, an adventure which inspired his next two travelogues, *The Silverado Squatters* and *The Amateur Emigrant*. And, of course, he went on to pen the novels which made him famous: *Treasure Island*, *The Strange Case of Dr Jekyll and Mr Hyde* and *Kidnapped*.

Although today best-known for his fiction, Stevenson was first and foremost a travel writer. Many critics consider him to be the 'father of modern travel writing', citing his honesty, humour and sensitive depictions of those he met *en route* – all too rare in the pompous milieu of late-Victorian literature. Perhaps Stevenson's best-known travel book is *Travels with a Donkey in the Cévennes* (1879), in which the author chronicles his twelve-day, 125-mile walk through the mountains of south-central France accompanied by an obstinate donkey he named Modestine. Before commencing this journey, Stevenson commissioned a roll of waterproof, wool-lined cart-cloth which he could use while camping outside – said to be the world's first purpose-made sleeping bag.

Hailed as a 'pioneering work of outdoor literature', *Travels with a Donkey* has motivated many latter-day hikers to retrace his steps along what is now the long-distance path, GR 70 – also known as *Chemin de Stevenson* (or 'Robert Louis Stevenson Trail'). But I like to think that his Cévennes expedition was inspired by an incident buried in 'In the Beechwoods', when the author was undertaking a much less challenging journey in the far gentler landscape of the English Chilterns four years earlier:

> After I had crossed the little zone of mist, the path began to remount the hill; and just as I, mounting along with it, had got back again, from the head downwards, into the thin golden sunshine, I saw in front of me a donkey tied to a tree. Now, I have a certain liking for donkeys…

The Conservationist

Unlike Robert Louis Stevenson, my Chiltern expedition did not end with a train journey to London, as my mother had offered to drive me on to College Lake, a nature reserve set in an old chalk quarry a few miles outside Tring. Opened to the public in 2010, it's now home to a thousand different wildlife species, including many wetland birds such as lapwing and redshank. It's also home to the Berks, Bucks & Oxon Wildlife Trust (BBOWT), and it was here that I'd arranged to meet Matthew Jackson, head of conservation at the organisation.

We sat down in the café, amid the clatter of crockery and the chatter of the kitchen staff. Over a cup of tea and a slice of cake I told Matthew about my journey across the Chilterns and my observations on the landscape I'd just walked through. I wanted to know his views on how the countryside had altered in the decades since I lived here, and the changes that HS2 would soon bring.

'Well, the wildlife changes since the 1970s have primarily been negative,' Matthew admitted. 'There are one or two positives – the reintroduction of red kites being the obvious one. But we've lost actual habitats. Grassland loss is the primary concern in the Chilterns.'

'It's been ploughed up?'

'Yes, but it's changing management as well. There are three habitats that the Chilterns are well known for. There are the chalk streams, there's the chalk grassland, and there's the beech woodland. In fact, they're not completely separate. You get overlaps between them – on some of our nicest sites, you get a mixture between woodland and grassland.' The Chilterns Matthew was describing was the Chilterns of my childhood memories.

'Has the landscape really changed so much in forty years?' I asked him.

'The losses really go back earlier than that – certainly post-war. The availability of fertiliser on a mass scale made a big difference. We lost quite a lot of pastureland to fertilisation of one sort or another. And that pretty much wipes out a lot of the wildlife in the chalk grass if you fertilise it.' It was only the day before that I was with Robert Brown in his Mitsubishi pick-up, bumping around an unimproved hay meadow clothed in clover and fertilised only by 'sheep poo'.

'What would you say are the main species that have suffered?' I asked. 'When I was walking over the Chilterns I was desperate to hear a skylark, but I didn't hear one for almost the whole three days. And then I heard what I'm pretty certain were skylarks, in a harvested field of oilseed rape. Is that a bird that has declined?'

'Yes, skylarks have declined pretty significantly over that period,' Matthew said. 'One of the issues with wildlife loss is that you can get a lot of decline before something goes extinct. We notice when it goes extinct, but we're not so good at noticing the declines. Farmland birds as a whole have all declined hugely. Skylarks are farmland birds.'

I'd always pictured skylarks in grassy meadows rather than humdrum farmland, so it was good to have it confirmed that I probably hadn't imagined them. Matthew went on to describe how other species such as butterflies and wildflowers had also declined in the previous forty years, and were now found only in small patches. Some had been lost through development – although the loss had been less in the Chilterns than other areas, partly due to the AONB's restrictive approach to planning. And while there had been some woodland loss the area was still relatively well-wooded, with some sites enjoying European protection as Special Areas of Conservation.

'How are these areas going to be affected by leaving the European Union?' I asked Matthew. As ever in such conversations nowadays, Brexit loomed large.

'Nobody knows, is the simple answer. The concern is that it becomes easier to weaken protection. At the moment we still have recourse to the European courts, which is something we had in relation to HS2. We were able to challenge the government's approach through the European system. Brexit changes that.' Post-Brexit, Matthew argued, if the government chose to do something that impacts on a nationally protected site, conservationists would have to prove that there's going to be damage. With European-protected sites the burden of proof is the other way around.

The conversation turned inescapably to HS2. I asked Matthew how he thought the train would affect wildlife in the Chilterns. He told me that although the route would go through two of BBOWT's nature reserves, Finemere Wood and Calvert Jubilee, the really important wildlife areas that would be hit by HS2 were mostly out of the Chilterns. Because of the tunnelling beneath much of the AONB, most of the hills and valleys wouldn't be largely or directly impacted – although tunnelling causes problems for chalk streams such as the Misbourne. According to Wikipedia's entry on the Misbourne:

> The river is a 'perch' stream, flowing over a bed of impermeable material on top of a porous substrate. This state is only quasi-stable, since in periods of low rainfall the water table drops below the level of the impermeable layer. If ground works are then carried out which damage this layer, the river can sink into the porous substrate and disappear.

Matthew explained what HS2 means for Chiltern chalk streams, such as the Misbourne. 'There's a lake south of here called Shardeloes Lake, which is lovely and very rich in wildlife. HS2 runs almost directly underneath. It's a chalk-stream fed lake, and so is obviously a significant site, but nobody quite knows whether there will be an impact or not. It's a question of which expert you believe in these cases. They are going to do things to try and limit the impact on the aquifer, but they don't know an awful lot about the geology underneath because it hasn't been fully investigated.'

'So your organisation has been campaigning, and you obviously feel strongly about it,' I said. 'Do you feel there's any more you can do, or do you feel it's a *fait accompli*?'

'It would take a small miracle for HS2 not to happen now,' Matthew replied. Not only had the government got parliamentary consent, with budget approval for phase one of the project from London to Birmingham, but they'd also spent vast sums acquiring land and on investigations. However, the original £56 billion cost was creeping up, with estimates putting phase one £204 million over budget. Some experts believe the first phase will cost £400 million per mile – almost twice the official figure and making it the most expensive railway ever built.

'With this level of government investment it would be a very brave politician who decided to backtrack on it,' Matthew concluded. His words reflected almost exactly those of Keith Hoffmeister a few days before. HS2 has its own momentum, even though you keep hearing arguments about how the economic case doesn't add up.

'It's like nobody wants to lose face, but wildlife and people will suffer,' I said.

'As an organisation we're not anti-train at all,' Matthew replied. 'Certainly in terms of transport initiatives, rail is generally much less damaging than roads. In terms of HS2, it's partly the methodology – the fact there weren't alternatives looked at – that led to important things not being known about. And the other issue with HS2, of course, is the high-speed nature of it.'

Matthew explained that most other trains can do much

more to avoid crucial areas because they can curve around them. But with the HS2 route, because of the need to maintain the velocity, any curve is enormously significant in terms of the impact it makes on the overall speed. So once the route of HS2 was chosen there was very little that could be done to vary it.

'I've read that HS2 would be faster than any train operating in Europe,' I added.

'That's right, and one of the problems with choosing to go with a high-speed option is that it limits the things you can do to mitigate the impact on sites. One of the other species that we've been particularly concerned about, because of the nature of the train, is the barn owl. Because they hunt flying at that height … well, you can imagine. It's a bit of a death-trap, basically.'

I told Matthew about a presentation on owls I had been to recently in Yorkshire. Apparently when the trains come past, the mice all run out because of the vibrations, and that's why hunting barn owls are hit by trains. HS2 Ltd themselves estimate that the train will result in the death of one percent of Britain's barn owls every year.

'And that's just train collisions,' said Matthew. 'There's also habitat loss and nest loss as part of the construction of the railway, but largely it's birds colliding with the trains.'

'So perhaps the electrification means there's a bigger impact?'

'Because of the width of track you need and the gantries that have to go in to accompany it. Now obviously, electric trains may be better for the environment in the grand scheme of things but in terms of the direct impact on the ground, it makes a difference.'

Matthew went on to explain that collisions of electric trains with birds and bats tended to be greater due to the pantograph extending the overall height of the structure, meaning the 'kinetic corridor' the train passes through is considerably larger for electric trains.

It was all very disheartening – and I wasn't even in the frontline of conservation, like Matthew Jackson.

'It must be quite difficult – I would even say depressing – doing your job,' I said. 'It must be hard to keep your chin up, as it were, when there's so much you're battling against.'

'Yes, but we do have some successes as well. For example, we were heavily involved in the discussions about just how much habitat should be created in relation to the habitats that are lost by HS2. Even in the twenty-odd years I've been working in nature conservation we've lost a lot. But what little we have left is much better protected than it used to be.'

The café had shut now, and the sun was setting over the lake. As our conversation drew to a close Matthew recommended I walk round the reserve, to watch the water birds gathering at sunset. Thanking him, I laced up my mud-caked boots one last time.

EPILOGUE

The Chiltern Chainsaw Massacre

It has been six months since I completed my Chiltern walk in the footsteps of Robert Louis Stevenson, and in the footprint of HS2. Or not quite completed it. On the second day of my journey, when I was about to cross the footprint of the railway as it will emerge from the tunnel at South Heath, my way was thwarted by works to the pylons marking the trajectory of the train through the Misbourne Valley. So today I've returned to complete the walk – around 200 metres of it, linking the footpath up from Great Missenden to South Heath at the top of the hill.

Much has happened in the intervening six months. Work on HS2 has begun at Euston Station, where the line is to terminate, with a local vicar padlocking herself to a doomed plane tree in Euston Square Gardens – a temporary construction site – highlighting the 'powerlessness and anger' that local people feel about the project. As in the Chilterns, London protesters have been tying knitted scarves around threatened trees, though it's not only trees that are under peril: around two hundred homes in the Camden area are due to be demolished to make way for the railway. Similar tree-chaining protests have been taking place at Hillingdon, an area of west London with a large tract of Green Belt, where campaigners have been opposing HS2's impact on trees and wildlife in the Colne Valley Park.

It's against this backdrop that I set out today, to place the final piece in my journey's jigsaw. Accompanying me is Keith Hoffmeister, whom I met before my walk last autumn and who probably knows more about the consequences of HS2 in the Chilterns than anyone else. Keith, who has not been back to South Heath since a winter sojourn in Australia, has offered to show me exactly where the tunnel portal will be built. It's a blustery spring day, a lull between late winter snowstorms, when we meet in Great Missenden, the epicentre of HS2's activities in the Chilterns. Taking our chances with the traffic, we dash across the A413 to the footpath leading out of the village and uphill to South Heath. This path is one of the many ancient routes connecting the settlements in the hollow of the Misbourne Valley with those on the plateau. Some routes, like nearby Frith Hill and Leather Lane, have become fully fledged roads in the intervening centuries. Others, like this one, have remained quiet paths for pedestrian traffic only.

The gate to the field and our footpath stops us – literally – in our tracks. 'WARNING', it announces in bright red lettering. 'PREMISES PROTECTED BY FORTEL SECURITY. 24hr DOG PATROL'. Alongside the words are pictures of an Alsatian dog and a CCTV camera, just in case you were in any doubt.

'This will be the construction compound for the temporary haul road, which was originally due to go up Leather and Bowood lanes,' Keith says as we enter the field. 'But because Stockings

Wood is ancient woodland, the haul road will skirt round to its left, up there. They'll have to remove quite a lot of soil, as the climb is so steep.'

Ahead of us, a large white van is parked up. A handful of workmen in orange hi-vis boiler suits are loitering outside. We cross the field to talk to them.

'All right?' they ask us as we approach.

'We're all right – how are you?' Keith responds with his customary cheeriness. 'So, what are you doing?'

'Not much at present,' one of the men replies. 'We're just waiting for the OK.'

'Who's going to give you the OK?' Keith asks. 'Is this something to do with HS2?'

'Yes, HS2,' the workman answers. 'This is part of the enabling works, to get the site ready. They're going to put a haul road up here, later this year.'

'So you're here to enable the enabling works?' quips Keith.

It turns out that the workmen, who have been here since eight this morning, are waiting for an ecologist to come down from 'up north somewhere' to check the hedge for nesting birds.

'They start the first of March, see, so we can't do anything without an ecologist,' the most talkative of the workmen explains. The beginning of March is when nesting has officially started, and the ecologist needs to investigate the hedge before giving the workmen the go-ahead to chop it down for the haul road. If he finds any nesting birds they have to leave a five-metre exclusion zone until nesting is finished.

'He's stuck in traffic, so we've been waiting three hours to begin,' says the workman, who seems to be enjoying the diversion.

'Yours are the first feet on the ground that we've seen here,' Keith says. Although these guys are only here to clear the vegetation where the haul road will go, he had expected, as a member of the Chiltern Society which has long been engaged in talks with HS2 Ltd, to have been informed of the work. It's obvious that this hedge-clearing has come as a surprise to him. He asks the men if he can take a photo of them all, as a memento.

'Quick, jump in the van, lads!' jokes the spokesman before they all pose cheerfully for Keith's camera. Photo taken, we leave them to their banter and continue up the hill. Although the exchanges were good-humoured, this is a sombre moment for Keith – and for me too.

'I wonder if, when they were building the railway here in the nineteenth century, people had the same sense of sadness at so much destruction, or whether they just welcomed it as "progress",' I muse.

'Well, the Victorian railway brought benefits to the community,' Keith replies. 'This railway isn't bringing any benefit to people in the Chilterns. It's just passing through, on the way to somewhere else. HS2 is no use to anyone here, or anyone who lives between London and Birmingham. In fact, it's doubtful it will be of use to anyone, anywhere.'

'Do you feel, seeing those guys with the chainsaws back there, that it's all too late for you to continue campaigning?' I quiz him.

'To stop it, maybe. But what we are trying to do is lessen the impact wherever possible.'

Soon, we're out of sight and sound of the workmen with their van and their eager chainsaws. We marvel at the sheer fluke of it, that our walk today just happened to coincide with HS2's first incision into the Chiltern Hills on this fine morning of proto-spring – six months on from the proto-autumn day I last walked here. The earth has revolved half way around the sun since then, from the autumn equinox to the spring equinox, and the theory of HS2 has now become a reality. So little has changed in the great, universal scheme of things, but so much has changed in this placid corner of the Chilterns. And so much more will change in the next few years for the people and the wildlife who call this place home.

As we approach Stockings Wood, birds chirping from treetops still wintry and skeletal, I spy three roe deer bounding away across the open fields. Their white tails bob as they run, like rabbits. A kite circles above the treetops, shrieking. Just ten minutes ago we were in crowded Middle England, with its traffic, its CCTV and its chainsaws. Here, as we reach the plateau, we are in wilderness filled with wildlife. Or at least, what passes for wilderness in the Chilterns. Keith notices bright red arrows painted on the grass beneath our feet, marking the route of the new haul road which will soon carry construction vehicles up this quiet hillside, and stops to take photos. Meanwhile, I pause to enjoy a moment of hush, and watch the deer grazing on pasture that will soon no longer exist.

Circumnavigating the crest of Stockings Wood, the trees fenced off with barbed wire, we return to the official public footpath to South Heath. Beech trees, some with their leaves still hanging and paper-dry, crackle in the cold spring wind. We reach the stile where I was halted six months ago, turned back by the pylon works. These same pylons mark the parallel course of HS2, which will pass alongside Jenkins Wood cutting an approximate hundred-metre wide gash into the landscape just where the three deer are now grazing. Although there will be a footbridge over the railway cutting when work is eventually completed, whether the wildlife of Stockings Wood and Jenkins Wood will benefit from it is highly doubtful.

The three deer have long gone by the time we cross the pasture to the arboreous sanctuary of Jenkins Wood. Lofty beeches, trunks as slender as supermodels, are the most prevalent species in this tract of 'semi-natural' ancient woodland. It's not only the trees that are ancient: Jenkins Wood hides earthworks which have been identified as a medieval motte and bailey, associated with the early manorial settlement that preceded the buildings at nearby Bury Farm. This must be the Moat and Enclosure on the map, and is one of six-thousand moated sites identified in England. According to Historic England, these consist of 'wide ditches, often or seasonally water-filled, partly or completely enclosing one or more islands of dry ground on which stood domestic or religious buildings'. The majority of moated sites were 'prestigious aristocratic and seigniorial residences with the provision of a moat intended as a status symbol rather than a practical military defence'. Most of England's moated sites were built between about 1250 and 1350, with the greatest concentration lying in central and eastern parts of England. Areas such as the Chilterns, then.

Although the cutting itself lies some seventy metres from Jenkins Wood, the activities of construction works will, according to the campaigners, endanger this historic monument. Disturbances in hydrology, noise, pollution and fragmentation of habitat are the main concerns. The cutting will also sever forever the link between Stockings and Jenkins woods, and the wildlife corridor they provide. As the ecologists Robert MacArthur and Edward O Wilson pointed out in their book *The Theory of Island Biogeography* (1967), the larger the 'islands' (or areas) of habitat, and the closer they are together, the better for wildlife. They also discovered that species will become extinct more readily on small 'islands' than large ones. So although there will be 'ecological mitigation sites' for relocated wildlife at Bury and Park Farms, they will not replace the lost habitats of ancient woodlands that have evolved over centuries.

'You can't repaint an old master,' says Keith as we trudge on through Jenkins Wood, still muddy after winter snowmelt. 'Well, you can try to repaint it, but then it won't be an old master.'

There's not much to see of the old motte and bailey from the footpath, just an overgrown earthwork which could be a later dell, or agricultural working. Soon, in a month or so, this wood will be carpeted with bluebells. Chiltern bluebells are not always the drooping, deep-purple native English variety (*Hyacinthoides non-scripta*), but often the taller, paler 'Spanish' hybrid invaders (*Hyacinthoides hispanica*) that have colonised much of England.

Leaving Keith to chat to a dog walker in the wood I cross the final field past Bury Farm to join the road through South Heath, and complete the final leg of my walk of six months earlier.

Bury: 'stronghold, fortified place'; from Old English *burh*, Proto-Germanic *byrgan*

The farmhouse itself dates back to the seventeenth century, when it was a manor house. But as its name suggests, the settlement is very much older. Archaeologists have discovered pottery on this site from the late Bronze and early Iron Ages, indicating early human occupation. It hides its antiquity behind a veneer of affluence, with its fresh coat of paint, dripping wisteria and indoor swimming pool housed in one of its weather-boarded barns. But this farmhouse, where the train is planned to pass within a hair's breadth, was bought by HS2 Ltd with £4.6 million of taxpayers' money and rented out to the ex-wife of a famous and troubled former footballer.

The stile onto the village road informs me that I'm on the Chiltern Heritage Trail. Opened in 2000 to celebrate the new millennium, this circular walk takes in some of the Chilterns' most characteristic towns and villages, such as the Chalfonts (St Peter and St Giles), Amersham and Great Missenden. It also passes through my own village of Ashley Green, almost directly opposite our house in Hog Lane. Before it became the Chiltern Heritage Trail, the bridleway crossing Hog Lane was the old coffin route from the outlying farms to the village church. I must have walked that path many times as a child, though not very far along it. Perhaps it seemed too dark, too hidden and mysterious to explore deeply. It's strange to find myself further along that same route so many decades later, though one soon to be mutilated by HS2.

The final link of my walk in place, I turn back to Jenkins Wood to find Keith. The wind blows softly and the sun shines hazily as we retrace our steps downhill towards Great Missenden.

We chat about the coincidences – the pylon works when I first walked here last autumn which led to my meeting the farmer Robert Brown, and which also prevented me from crossing the line of HS2 near Jenkins Wood. This in turn led to my walk today, and witnessing the first operation works of HS2 in the Chilterns. It almost feels like destiny.

Spying a chocolate wrapper blowing across the path I dutifully pick it up, even though a massive railway line will soon cut through here, devastating everything in its wake. Just as we emerge from Stockings Wood, halfway down the hill, the whine of machinery rises up from the valley bottom. Ahead, tiny figures in orange boiler suits are hacking at the hedgerow with their chainsaws, chucking the cut vegetation into a giant shredding machine. After the peace of our hilltop walk, with its birdsong and roe deer, the violence is shocking. The ecologist must have given the all-clear. In the half-hour since we were here, this old hedgerow has all but disappeared, leaving a gap the width of the new haul road. A swathe of hedgerow grown over centuries, and gone in minutes. As we near the workmen the whine of chainsaws grows louder.

Overhead – though I can barely hear it now – the faint squeal of a red kite. It is this once-vanished bird, rather than Stevenson's carolling skylarks, that had proved the most constant companion throughout my Chiltern journey in the footsteps of the author. To paraphrase him, 'the air was alive with them from High Wycombe to Tring'. Today of all days, the kite is a vital emblem of hope and renewal soaring high above the Chiltern Hills.

The Commuter

'I suppose you might say – to use a very old expression – I'm a rail enthusiast, in its broadest sense,' said John Elvin when I phoned him at his home in Winslow, Buckinghamshire. John is secretary of the Chiltern Line Association and a member of Railfuture, and has been an active campaigner for passengers' rights for the past thirty years. He is also one of the few local residents prepared to speak up for HS2.

John begun by telling me he was a retired chartered accountant who'd been in commerce virtually all his working life.

'It might surprise you to know that for the last sixteen years of my career I worked for a car company, Volkswagen at Milton Keynes,' he declared. 'So I have my feet in both camps in terms of what's better, rail or road.' Winslow, not far from Milton Keynes, is by all accounts a picturesque market town, first mentioned in 792 when King Offa gave it to St Albans Abbey. It lies in the Vale of Aylesbury, near the edge of the Chilterns and around five miles from where HS2 is planned to pass.

I asked John to tell me a little more about the Chiltern Line Association, and his work with the organisation.

'It goes back to the mid 1980s when British Rail, as it was then, planned to shut Marylebone Station, which meant that commuters in the Aylesbury/Great Missenden/Stoke

Mandeville/Amersham area would no longer be able to get a through train to London Marylebone,' John explained. 'In those days it was called the Aylesbury and District Railway Passengers Association, but a number of eminent people in Stoke Mandeville and other areas subsequently changed its name to the Chiltern Line Association.' Once Marylebone was reprieved in the late eighties the association turned from a purely campaigning group into one looking after passengers' rights.

'As secretary, I have quarterly meetings with Chiltern Railways where we have a board meeting with their managers,' John added, 'and we update them on any issues which need addressing in terms of the way the trains are being run.' Although not a rail commuter anymore, John is thus entitled to speak on their behalf, and expound on the potential benefits to commuters of HS2.

I kicked off the discussion by revealing that everybody I'd spoken to on my walk had said that the Chilterns was not going to benefit from HS2, complaining that the locals were going to suffer all the downsides of the railway and none of its upsides. So as a Chilterns' neighbour and a representative of Chiltern commuters, what in his opinion was the need for HS2? John was swift in his reply.

'One word – capacity. The present rail network, whether you go into Marylebone or into Euston or wherever, is running at total capacity at certain times of day. They simply cannot cram any more trains on to the existing tracks to get the people where they want to go. My daughter travels up from Leighton Buzzard into Euston and she has to sit on the floor of the train sometimes, because there's not enough room.'

'And the ticket prices are always going up as well,' I interjected.

'Exactly, so it doesn't get any better.' The rationale behind HS2, John told me, was to free up space on existing railways, principally the line into Euston. Currently, fifty percent of the rail lines into Euston are reserved for long-distance services from the Midlands and the North, where HS2 will go. 'So HS2 will release space on those lines so they can run more local trains for the ordinary commuters who can't get on the existing ones.'

I hadn't heard this argument before, but as he spoke it became apparent that John's position on HS2 was not as clear-cut as it first appeared.

'Although we strongly believe there is a need for a new rail link from London to the Midlands and the north, we feel the wrong route was chosen,' he continued. 'And unfortunately, we're now saddled with a route that passes through the Chiltern Hills.' John went on to tell me that this was due to a legacy from the then Labour government, specifying a route that went from London via Heathrow Airport to the Midlands – instead of the more direct route that ran parallel to the M1 motorway. Then, when the Heathrow spur was deleted from the plan, the route via the Chilterns was never revised.

'When they decided they didn't need the Heathrow link any longer, they could have easily changed the rest of it and paralleled a motorway – either the M40 or the M1 –

and could have got to Birmingham and the north that way,' said John. 'This would have caused far less consternation, and the people of the Chilterns would have been left in peace. But as they'd already designed the route through the Chilterns they thought they'd leave it as it was.'

I told John how I'd been reading about the history of HS2, and that the reason it was green-lighted was that David Cameron when prime minister promised there would be no third runway at Heathrow, and that HS2 was needed instead. 'Now, of course, there's going to be a third runway at Heathrow *and* HS2, so I suppose the question is whether it's still a necessary and viable line,' I added.

'Exactly. They said, we won't build a new runway at Heathrow, we'll divert HS2 to go via Heathrow – and that was to placate the people who said we must expand Heathrow.' And now, I reflected, it was the people and wildlife of the Chilterns who would have to live with this muddled policy decision.

'Given the local upset,' I ventured, 'what a pity they didn't extend the tunnel another few miles until it exited the AONB. People might then have been a bit happier about it.'

'Precisely – if they are going to spend all those billions on it, another six miles of tunnelling is hardly going to dent the overall budget much, is it?'

'Which is going up all the time, apparently.'

'Apparently so, yes.'

I then asked John whether, given the expanding costs of the railway, he thought it would actually materialise.

'At the moment I haven't heard any rumours or rumblings from the sources I keep in touch with that it's likely to be dropped,' was his reply. 'Construction is due to start in this area very shortly – they've done some preliminary work, installing electrical sub-stations and things like that, but there have been no spades in the ground yet. Once I see that, I think there'll probably be less chance of any turning back.'

Finally, and inevitably, the conversation turned to Brexit. I mentioned that some commentators were saying that after Brexit, particularly if we crashed out of the EU, the government might decide that they wouldn't have the money for this project. Did he agree? Or did he think they'd decide that they'd have to go ahead with it – if only to show that Britain was 'open for business'?

'My view on that is that if the political will is there, they will go ahead,' John replied. 'If we're seen to cut back on massive projects like HS2, it'll show that Britain is beginning to panic. The last thing you want is for international investors to see that Britain is panicking – that's from an accountant or investor point of view.'

We'd been talking for a good twenty minutes, and before ending the call I had a last question to put to John. On balance, given that HS2 has upset so many people in the Chilterns, and given it was not really fitting its original purpose to go via Heathrow, did he still think it was a good idea?

'Well, at the end of the day, it's not about getting to Birmingham fifteen minutes faster. As I say, it's about creating capacity on the rest of the network,' he responded. 'And if I can make just one more quick point ... people say, why build a high-speed line to Birmingham and the north? Why save ten minutes here and ten minutes there? The answer to that is, it's the modern way to build railways – you build them to a high-speed design. So we're not going to build them like the Victorians did, with lots of curves and swerves and things. That's the only reason they're building it high-speed. It's the modern way to do things – like Japan, with the Bullet Train.'

I thanked John for his time, and for expressing his views and those of the many Chiltern commuters he represents, on this most contentious of infrastructure projects. He had one last word on the subject.

'I have every sympathy for people living in and around the Chilterns, which I adore myself,' he said. 'But unless you're a rail traveller, you don't appreciate how crowded the existing rail network is. And until somebody comes up with a better idea, it seems we're stuck with HS2.'

IN THE BEECHWOODS

BY R L STEVENSON (1875)[1]

A country rapidly passed through under favourable auspices may leave upon us a unity of impression that would only be disturbed and dissipated if we stayed longer. Clear vision goes with the quick foot. Things fall for us into a sort of natural perspective when we see them for a moment in going by; we generalise boldly and simply, and are gone before the sun is overcast, before the rain falls, before the season can steal like a dial-hand from his figure, before the lights and shadows, shifting round towards nightfall, can show us the other side of things, and belie what they showed us in the morning. We expose our mind to the landscape (as we would expose the prepared plate in the camera) for the moment only during which the effect endures; and we are away before the effect can change. Hence we shall have in our memories a long

1 Although originally called 'In the Beechwoods', this essay was first published in *Portfolio* magazine in 1875 with the title 'An Autumn Effect'.

scroll of continuous wayside pictures, all imbued already with the prevailing sentiment of the season, the weather and the landscape, and certain to be unified more and more, as time goes on, by the unconscious processes of thought. So that we who have only looked at a country over our shoulder, so to speak, as we went by, will have a conception of it far more memorable and articulate than a man who has lived there all his life from a child upwards, and had his impression of to-day modified by that of to-morrow, and belied by that of the day after, till at length the stable characteristics of the country are all blotted out from him behind the confusion of variable effect.

I begin my little pilgrimage in the most enviable of all humours: that in which a person, with a sufficiency of money and a knapsack, turns his back on a town and walks forward into a country of which he knows only by the vague report of others. Such an one has not surrendered his will and contracted for the next hundred miles, like a man on a railway. He may change his mind at every finger-post, and, where ways meet, follow vague preferences freely and go the low road or the high, choose the shadow or the sun-shine, suffer himself to be tempted by the lane that turns immediately into the woods, or the broad road that lies open before him into the distance, and shows him the far-off spires of some city, or a range of mountain-tops, or a rim of sea, perhaps, along a low horizon. In short, he may gratify his every whim and fancy, without a pang of reproving conscience, or the least jostle to his self-respect. It is true, however, that most men do not possess the faculty of free action, the priceless gift of being able to live for the moment only; and as they begin to go forward on their journey, they will find that they have made for themselves new fetters. Slight projects they may have entertained for a moment, half in jest, become iron laws to them, they know not why. They will be led by the nose by these vague reports of which I spoke above; and the mere fact that their informant mentioned one village and not another will compel their footsteps with inexplicable power. And yet a little while, yet a few days of this fictitious liberty, and they will begin to hear imperious voices calling on them to return; and some passion, some duty, some worthy or unworthy expectation, will set its hand upon their shoulder and lead them back into the old paths. Once and again we have all made the experiment. We know the end of it right well. And yet if we make it for the hundredth time to-morrow: it will have the same charm as ever; our heart will beat and our eyes will be bright, as we leave the town behind us, and we shall feel once again (as we have felt so often before) that we are cutting ourselves loose for ever from our whole past life, with all its sins and follies and circumscriptions, and go forward as a new creature into a new world.

It was well, perhaps, that I had this first enthusiasm to encourage me up the long hill above High Wycombe; for the day was a bad day for walking at best, and now began to draw towards afternoon, dull, heavy, and lifeless. A pall of grey cloud covered the sky, and its colour reacted on the colour of the landscape. Near at hand, indeed, the hedgerow trees were still fairly green, shot through with bright autumnal yellows, bright as sunshine. But a little way off, the solid bricks of woodland that lay squarely on slope and hill-top were not green, but russet and grey, and ever less russet and more grey as they drew off into the distance. As they drew off into the distance, also, the woods seemed to mass themselves together, and lie thin and straight, like clouds, upon the limit of one's view. Not that this massing was complete, or gave the idea of any extent of forest, for every here and there the trees would break up and go down into a valley in open order, or stand in long Indian file along the horizon, tree after tree relieved, foolishly enough, against the sky. I say foolishly enough, although I have seen the effect employed cleverly in art, and such long line of single trees thrown out against the customary sunset of a Japanese picture with a certain fantastic effect that was not to be despised; but this was over water and level land, where it did not jar, as here, with the soft contour of hills and valleys. The whole scene had an indefinable look of being painted, the colour was so abstract and correct, and there was something so sketchy and merely impressional about these distant single trees on the horizon that one was forced to think of it all as of a clever French landscape. For it is rather in nature that we see resemblance to art, than in art to nature; and we say a hundred times, 'How like a picture!' for once that we say, 'How like the truth!' The forms in which we learn to think of landscape are forms that we have got from painted canvas. Any man can see and understand a picture; it is reserved for the few to separate anything out of the confusion of nature, and see that distinctly and with intelligence.

The sun came out before I had been long on my way; and as I had got by that time to the top of the ascent, and was now treading a labyrinth of confined by-roads, my whole view brightened considerably in colour, for it was the distance only that was grey and cold, and the distance I could see no longer. Overhead there was a wonderful carolling of larks which seemed to follow me as I went. Indeed, during all the time I was in that country the larks did not desert me. The air was alive with them from High Wycombe to Tring; and as, day after day, their 'shrill delight' fell upon me out of the vacant sky, they began to take such a prominence over other conditions, and form so integral a part of my conception of the country, that I could have baptized it 'The Country of Larks'. This, of course, might just as well have been in early spring; but everything else was deeply imbued with the sentiment of the later year. There was no stir of insects in the grass. The sunshine was more golden, and gave less heat than summer sunshine; and the shadows under the hedge were somewhat blue and misty. It was only in autumn that you could have seen the mingled green and yellow of the elm foliage, and the fallen leaves that lay about the road, and covered the surface of wayside pools so thickly that the sun was reflected only here and there from little joints and pinholes in that brown coat of proof; or that your ear would have been troubled, as you went forward, by the occasional report of fowling-pieces from all directions and all degrees of distance.

For a long time this dropping fire was the one sign of human activity that came to disturb me as I walked. The lanes were profoundly still. They would have been sad but for the sunshine and the singing of the larks. And as it was, there came over me at times a feeling of isolation that was not disagreeable, and yet was enough to make me quicken my steps eagerly when I saw some one before me on the road. This fellow-voyager proved to be no less a person than the parish constable. It had occurred to me that in a district which was so little populous and so well wooded, a criminal of any intelligence might play hide-and-seek with the authorities for months; and this idea was strengthened by the aspect of the portly constable as he walked by my side with deliberate dignity and turned-out toes. But a few minutes' converse set my heart at rest. These rural criminals are very tame birds, it appeared. If my informant did not immediately lay his hand on an offender, he was content to wait; some evening after nightfall there would come a tap at his door, and the outlaw, weary of outlawry, would give himself quietly up to undergo sentence, and resume his position in the life of the countryside. Married men caused him no disquietude whatever; he had them fast by the foot. Sooner or later they would come back to see their wives, a peeping neighbour would pass the word, and my portly constable would walk quietly over and take the bird sitting. And if there were a few who had no particular ties in the neighbourhood, and preferred to shift into another county when they fell into trouble, their departure moved the placid constable in no degree. He was of Dogberry's opinion; and if a man would not stand in the Prince's name, he took no note of him, but let him go, and thanked God he was rid of a knave. And surely the crime and the law were in admirable keeping; rustic constable was well met with rustic offender. The officer sitting at home over a bit of fire until the criminal came to visit him, and the criminal coming – it was a fair match. One felt as if this must have been the order in that delightful seaboard Bohemia where Florizel and Perdita courted in such sweet accents, and the Puritan sang Psalms to hornpipes, and the four-and-twenty shearers danced with nosegays in their bosoms, and chanted their three songs apiece at the old shepherd's festival; and one could not help picturing to oneself what havoc among good peoples purses, and tribulation for benignant constables, might be worked here by the arrival, over stile and footpath, of a new Autolycus.

Bidding good-morning to my fellow-traveller, I left the road and struck across country. It was rather a revelation to pass from between the hedgerows and find quite a bustle on the other side, a great coming and going of school-children upon by-paths, and, in every second field, lusty horses and stout country-folk a-ploughing. The way I followed took me through many fields thus occupied, and through many strips of plantation, and then over a little space of smooth turf, very pleasant to the feet, set with tall fir-trees and clamorous with rooks making ready for the winter, and so back again into the quiet road. I was now not far from the end of my day's journey. A few hundred yards farther, and, passing through a gap in the hedge, I began to go down hill through a pretty extensive tract of young beeches. I was soon in shadow myself, but the afternoon sun still coloured the upmost boughs of the wood, and made a fire over my head in the autumnal foliage. A little faint vapour lay among the slim tree-stems in the bottom of the hollow; and from farther up I heard from time to time an outburst of gross laughter, as though clowns were making merry in the bush. There was something about the atmosphere that brought all sights and sounds home to one with a singular purity, so that I felt as if my senses had been washed with water. After I had crossed the little zone of mist, the path began to remount the hill; and just as I, mounting along with it, had got back again, from the head downwards, into the thin golden sunshine, I saw in front of me a donkey tied to a tree. Now, I have a certain liking for donkeys, principally, I believe, because of the delightful things that Sterne has written of them. But this was not after the pattern of the ass at Lyons. He was of a white colour, that seemed to fit him rather for rare festal occasions than for constant drudgery.

Besides, he was very small, and of the daintiest portions you can imagine in a donkey. And so, sure enough, you had only to look at him to see he had never worked. There was something too roguish and wanton in his face, a look too like that of a schoolboy or a street Arab, to have survived much cudgelling. It was plain that these feet had kicked off sportive children oftener than they had plodded with a freight through miry lanes. He was altogether a fine-weather, holiday sort of donkey; and though he was just then somewhat solemnised and rueful, he still gave proof of the levity of his disposition by impudently wagging his ears at me as I drew near. I say he was somewhat solemnised just then; for, with the admirable instinct of all men and animals under restraint, he had so wound and wound the halter about the tree that he could go neither back nor forwards, nor so much as put down his head to browse. There he stood, poor rogue, part puzzled, part angry, part, I believe, amused. He had not given up hope, and dully revolved the problem in his head, giving ever and again another jerk at the few inches of free rope that still remained unwound. A humorous sort of sympathy for the creature took hold upon me. I went up, and, not without some trouble on my part, and much distrust and resistance on the part of Neddy, got him forced backwards until the whole length of the halter was set loose, and he was once more as free a donkey as I dared to make him. I was pleased (as people are) with this friendly action to a fellow-creature in tribulation, and glanced back over my shoulder to see how he was profiting by his freedom. The brute was looking after me; and no sooner did he catch my eye than he put up his long white face into the air, pulled an impudent mouth at me, and began to bray derisively. If ever any one person made a grimace at another, that donkey made a grimace at me. The hardened ingratitude of his behaviour, and the impertinence that inspired his whole face as he curled up his lip, and showed his teeth, and began to bray, so tickled me, and was so much in keeping with what I had imagined to myself about his character, that I could not find it in my heart to be angry, and burst into a peal of hearty laughter. This seemed to strike the ass as a repartee, so he brayed at me again by way of rejoinder; and we went on for a while, braying and laughing, until I began to grow aweary of it, and, shouting a derisive farewell, turned to pursue my way. In so doing – it was like going suddenly into cold water – I found myself face to face with a prim little old maid. She was all in a flutter, the poor old dear! She had concluded beyond question that this must be a lunatic who stood laughing aloud at a white donkey in the placid beech-woods. I was sure, by her face, that she had already recommended her spirit most religiously to Heaven, and prepared herself for the worst. And so, to reassure her, I uncovered and besought her, after a very staid fashion, to put me on my way to Great Missenden. Her voice trembled a little, to be sure, but I think her mind was set at rest; and she told me, very explicitly, to follow the path until I came to the end of the wood, and then I should see the village below me in the bottom of the valley. And, with mutual courtesies, the little old maid and I went on our respective ways.

Nor had she misled me. Great Missenden was close at hand, as she had said, in the trough of a gentle valley, with many great elms about it. The smoke from its chimneys went up pleasantly in the afternoon sunshine. The sleepy hum of a threshing-machine filled the neighbouring fields and hung about the quaint street corners. A little above, the church sits well back on its haunches against the hillside – an attitude for a church, you know, that makes it look as if it could be ever so much higher if it liked; and the trees grew about it thickly, so as to make a density of shade in the churchyard. A very quiet place it looks; and yet I saw many boards and posters about threatening dire punishment against those who broke the church windows or defaced the precinct, and offering rewards for the apprehension of those who had done the like already. It was fair day in Great Missenden. There were three stalls set up, *sub jove*, for the sale of pastry and cheap toys; and a great number of holiday children thronged about the stalls and noisily invaded every corner of the straggling village. They came round me by coveys, blowing simultaneously upon penny trumpets as though they imagined I should fall to pieces like the battlements of Jericho. I noticed one among them who could make a wheel of himself like a London boy, and seemingly enjoyed a grave pre-eminence upon the strength of the accomplishment. By and by, however, the trumpets began to weary me, and I went indoors, leaving the fair, I fancy, at its height.

Night had fallen before I ventured forth again. It was pitch-dark in the village street, and the darkness seemed only the greater for a light here and there in an uncurtained window or from an open door. Into one such window I was rude enough to peep, and saw within a charming *genre* picture. In a room, all white wainscot and crimson wall-paper, a perfect gem of colour after the black, empty darkness in which I had been groping, a pretty girl was telling a story, as well as I could make out, to an attentive child upon her knee, while an old woman sat placidly dozing over the fire. You may be sure I was not behindhand with a story for myself – a good old story after the manner of G. P. R. James and the village melodramas, with a wicked squire, and poachers, and an attorney, and a virtuous young man with a genius for mechanics, who should love, and protect, and ultimately marry the girl in the crimson room. Baudelaire has a few dainty sentences on the fancies that we are inspired with when we look through a window into other people's lives; and I think Dickens has somewhere enlarged on the same text. The subject, at least, is one that I am seldom weary of entertaining. I remember, night after night, at Brussels, watching a good family sup together, make merry, and retire to rest; and night after night I waited to see the candles lit, and the salad made, and the last salutations dutifully exchanged, without any abatement of interest. Night after night I found the scene rivet my attention and keep me awake in bed with all manner of quaint imaginations. Much of the pleasure of the *Arabian Nights* hinges upon this Asmodean interest; and we are not weary of lifting other people's roofs, and going about behind the scenes of life with the Caliph and the serviceable Giaffar. It is a salutary exercise, besides; it is salutary to get out of ourselves and see people living together in perfect unconsciousness of our existence, as they will live when we are gone. If to-morrow the blow falls, and the worst of our ill fears is realised, the girl will none the less tell stories to the child on her lap in the cottage at Great Missenden, nor the good Belgians light their candle, and mix their salad, and go orderly to bed.

The next morning was sunny overhead and damp underfoot, with a thrill in the air like a reminiscence of frost. I went up into the sloping garden behind the inn and smoked a pipe pleasantly enough, to the tune of my landlady's lamentations over sundry cabbages and cauliflowers that had been spoiled by caterpillars.

She had been so much pleased in the summer-time, she said, to see the garden all hovered over by white butterflies. And now, look at the end of it! She could nowise reconcile this with her moral sense. And, indeed, unless these butterflies are created with a side-look to the composition of improving apologues, it is not altogether easy, even for people who have read Hegel and Dr. M'Cosh, to decide intelligibly upon the issue raised. Then I fell into a long and abstruse calculation with my landlord; having for object to compare the distance driven by him during eight years' service on the box of the Wendover coach with the girth of the round world itself. We tackled the question most conscientiously, made all necessary allowance for Sundays and leap-years, and were just coming to a triumphant conclusion of our labours when we were stayed by a small lacuna in my information. I did not know the circumference of the earth. The landlord knew it, to be sure – plainly he had made the same calculation twice and once before – but he wanted confidence in his own figures, and from the moment I showed myself so poor a second seemed to lose all interest in the result.

Wendover (which was my next stage) lies in the same valley with Great Missenden, but at the foot of it, where the hills trend off on either hand like a coast-line, and a great hemisphere of plain lies, like a sea, before one, I went up a chalky road, until I had a good outlook over the place. The vale, as it opened out into the plain, was shallow, and a little bare, perhaps, but full of graceful convolutions. From the level to which I have now attained the fields were exposed before me like a map, and I could see all that bustle of autumn field-work which had been hid from me yesterday behind the hedgerows, or shown to me only for a moment as I followed the footpath. Wendover lay well down in the midst, with mountains of foliage about it. The great plain stretched away to the northward, variegated near at hand with the quaint pattern of the fields, but growing ever more and more indistinct, until it became a mere hurly-burly of trees and bright crescents of river, and snatches of slanting road, and finally melted into the ambiguous cloud-land over the horizon. The sky was an opal-grey, touched here and there with blue, and with certain faint russets that looked as if they were reflections of the colour of the autumnal woods below. I could hear the ploughmen shouting to their horses, the uninterrupted carol of larks innumerable overhead, and, from a field where the shepherd was marshalling his flock, a sweet tumultuous tinkle of sheep-bells. All these noises came to me very thin and distinct in the clear air. There was a wonderful sentiment of distance and atmosphere about the day and the place.

I mounted the hill yet farther by a rough staircase of chalky footholds cut in the turf. The hills about Wendover and, as far as I could see, all the hills in Buckinghamshire, wear a sort of hood of beech plantation; but in this particular case the hood had been suffered to extend itself into something more like a cloak, and hung down about the shoulders of the hill in wide folds, instead of lying flatly along the summit. The trees grew so close, and their boughs were so matted together, that the whole wood looked as dense as a bush of heather. The prevailing colour was a dull, smouldering red, touched here and there with vivid yellow. But the autumn had scarce advanced beyond the outworks; it was still almost summer in the heart of the wood; and as soon as I had scrambled through the hedge, I found myself in a dim green forest atmosphere under eaves of virgin foliage. In places where the wood had itself for a background and the trees were massed together thickly, the colour became intensified and almost gem-like: a perfect fire green, that seemed none the less green for a few specks of autumn gold. None of the trees were of any considerable age or stature; but they grew well together, I have said; and as the road turned and wound among them, they fell into pleasant groupings and broke the light up pleasantly. Sometimes there would be a colonnade of slim, straight tree-stems with the light running down them as down the shafts of pillars, that looked as if it ought to lead to something, and led only to a corner of sombre and intricate jungle. Sometimes a spray of delicate foliage would be thrown out flat, the light lying flatly along the top of it, so that against a dark background it seemed almost luminous. There was a great bush over the thicket (for, indeed, it was more of a thicket than a wood); and the vague rumours that went among the tree-tops, and the occasional rustling of big birds or hares among the undergrowth, had in them a note of almost treacherous stealthiness, that put the imagination on its guard and made me walk warily on the russet carpeting of last year's leaves. The spirit of the place seemed to be all attention; the wood listened as I went, and held its breath to number my footfalls. One could not help feeling that there ought to be some reason for this stillness; whether, as the bright old legend goes, Pan lay somewhere near in siesta, or whether, perhaps, the heaven was meditating rain, and the first drops would soon come pattering through the leaves. It was not unpleasant, in such an humour, to catch sight, ever and anon, of large spaces of the open plain. This happened only where the path lay much upon the slope, and there was a flaw in the solid leafy thatch of the wood at some distance below the level at which I chanced myself to be walking; then, indeed, little scraps of foreshortened distance, miniature fields, and Lilliputian houses and hedgerow trees would appear for a moment in the aperture, and grow larger and smaller, and change and melt one into another, as I continued to go forward, and so shift my point of view.

For ten minutes, perhaps, I had heard from somewhere before me in the wood a strange, continuous noise, as of clucking, cooing, and gobbling, now and again interrupted by a harsh scream. As I advanced towards this noise, it began to grow lighter about me, and I caught sight, through the trees, of sundry gables and enclosure walls, and something like the tops of a rickyard. And sure enough, a rickyard it proved to be, and a neat little farm-steading, with the beech-woods growing almost to the door of it. Just before me, however, as I came upon the path, the trees drew back and let in a wide flood of daylight on to a circular lawn. It was here that the noises had their origin. More than a score of peacocks (there are altogether thirty at the farm), a proper contingent of peahens, and a great multitude that I could not number of more ordinary barn-door fowls, were all feeding together on this little open lawn among the beeches. They fed in a dense crowd, which swayed to and fro, and came hither and thither as by a sort of tide, and of which the surface was agitated like the surface of a sea as each bird guzzled his head along the ground after the scattered corn. The clucking, cooing noise that had led me thither was formed by the blending together of countless expressions of individual contentment into one collective expression of contentment, or general grace during meat. Every now and again a big peacock would separate himself from the mob and take a stately turn or two about the lawn, or perhaps mount for a moment upon the rail, and there shrilly publish to the world his satisfaction with himself and what he had to eat. It happened, for my sins, that none of these admirable birds had anything beyond the merest rudiment of a tail. Tails, it seemed, were out of season just then. But they had their necks for all that; and by their necks alone they do as much surpass all the other birds of our grey climate as they fall in quality of song below the blackbird or the lark. Surely the peacock, with its incomparable parade of glorious colour and the scannel voice of it issuing forth, as in mockery, from its painted throat, must, like my landlady's butterflies at Great Missenden, have been invented by some skilful fabulist for the consolation and support of homely virtue: or rather, perhaps, by a fabulist not quite so skilful, who made points for the moment without having a studious enough eye to the complete effect; for I thought these melting greens and blues so beautiful that afternoon, that I would have given them my vote just then before the sweetest pipe in all the spring woods. For indeed there is no piece of colour of the same extent in nature, that will so flatter and satisfy the lust of a man's eyes; and to come upon so many of them, after these acres of stone-coloured heavens and russet woods, and grey-brown ploughlands and white roads, was like going three whole days' journey to the southward, or a month back into the summer.

I was sorry to leave *Peacock Farm* – for so the place is called, after the name of its splendid pensioners – and go forwards again in the quiet woods. It began to grow both damp and dusk under the beeches; and as the day declined the colour faded out of the foliage; and shadow, without form and void, took the place of all the fine tracery of leaves and delicate gradations of living green that had before accompanied my walk. I had been sorry to leave *Peacock Farm*, but I was not sorry to find myself once more in the open road, under a pale and somewhat troubled-looking evening sky, and put my best foot foremost for the inn at Wendover.

Wendover, in itself, is a straggling, purposeless sort of place. Everybody seems to have had his own opinion as to how the street should go; or rather, every now and then a man seems to have arisen with a new idea on the subject, and led away a little sect of neighbours to join in his heresy. It would have somewhat the look of an abortive watering-place, such as we may now see them here and there along the coast, but for the age of the houses, the comely quiet design of some of them, and the look of long habitation, of a life that is settled and rooted, and makes it worth while to train flowers about the windows, and otherwise shape the dwelling to the humour of the inhabitant. The church, which might perhaps have served as rallying-point for these loose houses, and pulled the township into something like intelligible unity, stands some distance off among great trees; but the inn (to take the public buildings in order of importance) is in what I understand to be the principal street: a pleasant old house, with bay-windows, and three peaked gables, and many swallows' nests plastered about the eaves.

The interior of the inn was answerable to the outside: indeed, I never saw any room much more to be admired than the low wainscoted parlour in which I spent the remainder of the evening. It was a short oblong in shape, save that the fireplace was built across one of the angles so as to cut it partially off, and the opposite angle was similarly truncated by a corner cupboard. The wainscot was white, and there was a Turkey carpet on the floor, so old that it might have been imported by Walter Shandy before he retired, worn almost through in some places, but in others making a good show of blues and oranges, none the less harmonious for being somewhat faded. The corner cupboard was agreeable in design; and there were just the right things upon the shelves – decanters and tumblers, and blue plates, and one red rose in a glass of water. The furniture was old-fashioned and stiff. Everything was in keeping, down to the ponderous leaden inkstand on the round table. And you may fancy how pleasant it looked, all flushed and flickered over by the light of a brisk companionable fire, and seen, in a strange, tilted sort of perspective, in the three compartments of the old mirror above the chimney. As I sat reading in the great armchair, I kept looking round with the tail of my eye at the quaint, bright picture that was about me, and could not help some pleasure and a certain childish pride in forming part of it. The book I read was about Italy in the early Renaissance, the pageantries and the light loves of princes, the passion of men for learning, and poetry, and art; but it was written, by good luck, after a solid, prosaic fashion, that suited the room infinitely more nearly than the matter; and the result was that I thought less, perhaps, of Lippo Lippi, or Lorenzo, or Politian, than of the good Englishman who had written in that volume what he knew of them, and taken so much pleasure in his solemn polysyllables.

I was not left without society. My landlord had a very pretty little daughter, whom we shall call Lizzie. If I had made any notes at the time, I might be able to tell you something definite of her appearance. But faces have a trick of growing more and more spiritualised and abstract in the memory, until nothing remains of them but a look, a haunting expression; just that secret quality in a face that is apt to slip out somehow under the cunningest painter's touch, and leave the portrait dead for the lack of it. And if it is hard to catch with the finest of camel's-hair pencils, you may think how hopeless it must be to pursue after it with clumsy words. If I say, for instance, that this look, which I remember as Lizzie, was something wistful that seemed partly to come of slyness and in part of simplicity, and that I am inclined to imagine it had something to do with the daintiest suspicion of a cast in one of her large eyes, I shall have said all that I can, and the reader will not be much advanced towards comprehension. I had struck up an acquaintance with this little damsel in the morning, and professed much interest in her dolls, and an impatient desire to see the large one which was kept locked away for great occasions. And so I had not been very long in the parlour before the door opened, and in came Miss Lizzie with two dolls tucked clumsily under her arm. She was followed by her brother John, a year or so younger than herself, not simply to play propriety at our interview, but to show his own two whips in emulation of his sister's dolls. I did my best to make myself agreeable to my visitors, showing much admiration for the dolls and dolls' dresses, and, with a very serious demeanour, asking many questions about their age and character. I do not think that Lizzie distrusted my sincerity, but it was evident that she was both bewildered and a little contemptuous. Although she was ready herself to treat her dolls as if they were alive, she seemed to think rather poorly of any grown person who could fall heartily into the spirit of the fiction. Sometimes she would look at me with gravity and a sort of disquietude, as though she really feared I must be out of my wits. Sometimes, as when I inquired too particularly into the question of their names, she laughed at me so long and heartily that I began to feel almost embarrassed. But when, in an evil moment, I asked to be allowed to kiss one of them, she could keep herself no longer to herself. Clambering down from the chair on which she sat perched to show me, Cornelia-like, her jewels, she ran straight out of the room and into the bar – it was just across the passage – and I could hear her telling her mother in loud tones, but apparently more in sorrow than in merriment, that *the gentleman in the parlour wanted to kiss dolly*. I fancy she was determined to save me from this humiliating action, even in spite of myself, for she never gave me the desired permission. She reminded me of an old dog I once knew, who would never suffer the master of the house to dance, out of an exaggerated sense of the dignity of that master's place and carriage.

After the young people were gone there was but one more incident ere I went to bed. I heard a party of children go up and down the dark street for a while, singing together sweetly. And the mystery of this little incident was so pleasant to me that I purposely refrained from asking who they were, and wherefore they went singing at so late an hour. One can rarely be in a pleasant place without meeting with some pleasant accident. I have a conviction that these children would not have gone singing before the inn unless the inn-parlour had been the delightful place it was. At least, if I had been in the customary public room of the modern hotel, with all its disproportions and discomforts, my ears would have been dull, and there would have been some ugly temper or other uppermost in my spirit, and so they would have wasted their songs upon an unworthy hearer.

Next morning I went along to visit the church. It is a long-backed red-and-white building, very much restored, and stands in a pleasant graveyard among those great trees of which I have spoken already. The sky was drowned in a mist. Now and again pulses of cold wind went about the enclosure, and set the branches busy overhead, and the dead leaves scurrying into the angles of the church buttresses. Now and again, also, I could hear the dull sudden fall of a chestnut among the grass – the dog would bark before the rectory door – or there would come a clinking of pails from the stable-yard behind. But in spite of these occasional interruptions – in spite, also, of the continuous autumn twittering that filled the trees – the chief impression somehow was one as of utter silence, insomuch that the little greenish bell that peeped out of a window in the tower disquieted me with a sense of some possible and more inharmonious disturbance. The grass was wet, as if with a hoar frost that had just been melted. I do not know that ever I saw a morning more autumnal. As I went to and fro among the graves, I saw some flowers set reverently before a recently erected tomb, and drawing near, was almost startled to find they lay on the grave a man seventy-two years old when he died. We are accustomed to strew flowers only over the young, where love has been cut short untimely, and great possibilities have been restrained by death. We strew them there in token, that these possibilities, in some deeper sense, shall yet be realised, and the touch of our dead loves remain with us and guide us to the end. And yet there was more significance, perhaps, and perhaps a greater consolation, in this little nosegay on the grave of one who had died old. We are apt to make so much of the tragedy of death, and think so little of the enduring tragedy of some men's lives, that we see more to lament for in a life cut off in the midst of usefulness and love, than in one that miserably survives all love and usefulness, and goes about the world the phantom of itself, without hope, or joy, or any consolation. These flowers seemed not so much the token of love that survived death, as of something yet more beautiful – of love that had lived a man's life out to an end with him, and been faithful and companionable, and not weary of loving, throughout all these years.

The morning cleared a little, and the sky was once more the old stone-coloured vault over the sallow meadows and the russet woods, as I set forth on a dog-cart from Wendover to Tring. The road lay for a good distance along the side of the hills, with the great plain below on one hand, and the beech-woods above on the other. The fields were busy with people ploughing and sowing; every here and there a jug of ale stood in the angle of the hedge, and I could see many a team wait smoking in the furrow as ploughman or sower stepped aside for a moment to take a draught. Over all the brown ploughlands, and under all the leafless hedgerows, there was a stout piece of labour abroad, and, as it were, a spirit of picnic. The horses smoked and the men laboured and shouted and drank in the sharp autumn morning; so that one had a strong effect of large, open-air existence. The fellow who drove me was something of a humourist; and his conversation was all in praise of an agricultural labourer's way of life. It was he who called my attention to these jugs of ale by the hedgerow; he could not sufficiently express the liberality of these men's wages; he told me how sharp an appetite was given by breaking up the earth in the morning air, whether with plough or spade, and cordially admired this provision of nature. He sang *O Fortunatos Agricolas!* indeed, in every possible key, and with many cunning inflections, till I began to wonder what was the use of such people as Mr. Arch, and to sing the same air myself in a more diffident manner.

Tring was reached, and then Tring railway-station; for the two are not very near, the good people of Tring having held the railway, of old days, in extreme apprehension, lest some day it should break loose in the town and work mischief. I had a last walk, among russet beeches as usual, and the air filled, as usual, with the carolling of larks; I heard shots fired in the distance, and saw, as a new sign of the fulfilled autumn, two horsemen exercising a pack of fox-hounds. And then the train came and carried me back to London.

Requiem

Under the wide and starry sky
Dig the grave and let me lie.
Glad did I live and gladly die,
And I laid me down with a will.

This be the verse you 'grave for me;
'Here he lies where he long'd to be,
Home is the sailor, home from sea,
And the hunter home from the hill.'

Epitaph by R L Stevenson, carved on his hill-top grave in Samoa

INDEX

of People and Local Place Names

Buckland
Aston Clinton
Aston Clinton Park
Rye Green
Lodge Farm
Halton
Aston Hill
Astonhill Farm
Acres 3809·270
Acres 1455·877
Ballad's Wood
Halton Wood
WENDOVER
The Hale
Hale Wood
Cock's Hill
Acres
W E N D O V E R